Grace & Peace

Pastor Bob

Tough Love

by

Rev. Robert D. Culbertson

Author's note: All references herein to "Mission" mean the Door of Faith Mission in Des Moines, Iowa. For reasons of privacy, the real names of the residents of the Mission have not been used.

Copyright © 2007
by Rev. Robert D. Culbertson

Robert D. Culbertson
6222 University Avenue
Des Moines, IA 50311

www.WindsorChurch.com

Printed in the U.S. by InstantPublisher.com
ISBN 978-1-60458-122-5

Table of Contents

Foreword

I was born and reared in a small community in northeast Iowa. My parents operated a dairy farm outside of Edgewood. Spending the first 18 years of my life, morning and evening, in the dairy barn was a fairly good motivator for me to try other things in life. I also want to thank both my parents for being insistent that I attend college after graduating from high school. I know that my dad would have dearly loved to have been able to attend college but it was expected back then that he would continue farming with his parents.

There were many benefits for a young child being reared on a farm but free time was not one of those benefits. I recall in second grade having my folks call me out to the barn one evening. I had expected to be in trouble for skipping chores that night only to find that in one of the stalls was a new pony and colt waiting for me. In the coming years the horses and I would be inseparable. I graduated in 1971 from Edgewood-Colesburg High School. As in many small schools in rural Iowa, you knew everyone in your class and it was easy to be involved in different activities at school.

In order to help my parents on the farm, I decided to attend Upper Iowa College, located in Fayette, Iowa, which was about 35 miles from home. I would graduate from there with a double major: History was one major and the study of it would be a love that I have maintained over the years. I also majored in Religion-Philosophy, which would assist me in seminary and in the church. It was during my college years that I began to develop a positive self image, in part thanks to two professors who had a dramatic impact upon my life. Doc Wilcox and Dean Gill would show me what a tremendous effect people have upon the direction of one's life if we only choose to take the time needed to connect with others on this journey.

My father had heart problems during this time and I decided to attend seminary in Dubuque in order to help him on the farm while he recuperated from the heart attack. I would graduate from the University of Dubuque Theological Seminary with my Master of Divinity in 1978. It was during this time I also had a small non-denominational church and began to realize how God might use me in the coming years. The congregation was very forgiving and loving as I look back on the three and one-half years we shared together.

In 1978 I was appointed to the First United Methodist Church in Boone, Iowa, as the associate pastor and served there for the next three years. The last year there I also served the Marion Street United Methodist Church in Boone as its pastor, along with my appointment to Boone First.

The next nine years I was part of the folks' lives in Dallas Center as God allowed me to be their pastor. We all have places where we grow up and that was one such place for me. Many of those folks remain close to my heart even today.

Starting in 1990, until January of 1993, I served as the associate pastor at Aldersgate United Methodist Church in Des Moines. During this time I began to feel the need to do something different in my life. A friend of mine had been serving as the Sky Walk Chaplain for the past several years but was forced to retire due to poor health. He suggested that I might enjoy this, as he had, and that I should apply. Over the next ten and one-half years, I was connected to the Door of Faith Mission–serving in different roles as my job developed.

The stories in this book and the way those experiences changed my life are a direct result of those years. I hope you enjoy them and that you may hear God through them, just as I have felt God's presence. They are more than stories about men who happened to be at the

Mission during those years. They are experiences through which God spoke to me and showed me things about my life and how I might share my life with those who God guided across my path. Those men were such a blessing to me and my family, I can only pray that I might have touched them positively in some small way.

Julie and I decided in 2004 that it was time to return to the local church. We hoped to share much of what we have learned with those in our faith community. God blessed us by calling us to serve the congregation located at 63rd and University Avenue, in Des Moines, known as Windsor United Methodist Church. It is truly a blessed community of faith. The congregation, like many of the churches I have been called to serve, endures my stories and continues to help me develop into the person God has called me to be.

Acknowledgments

I have a terrible habit of skipping certain parts of any book I find myself picking up to read. I can't ever remember a time when I have read the acknowledgment section until recently. The past year that I have been working on this manuscript has been a truly blessed event in my life. I would never have taken the time nor expended the effort had it not been for a member of my church. Max and Liz Isaacson had my wife, Julie, and me over for dinner one evening. As we visited, I found myself sharing stories about the Door of Faith Mission and some of the ways the men had touched our lives.

It was several weeks later that a package arrived at my office. Max sent me six pages of material in which he outlined ways for me to record my stories and have them published. He offered to edit and help me publish the material if I were willing to do so. I can't begin to thank him enough for his encouragement and support. Merely recalling those times has been such a blessing in my life. An added benefit has been getting to know Max personally as well. Thank you, Max, for encouraging me and supporting me. We have agreed that any profit from the sale of this book will go to the budget which supports mission trips for our church. Any way I can encourage others to experience what I have received from God is what I hope to gain from this endeavor.

I want to thank Julie for keeping me grounded. She has continually challenged me to tell only the story and not to embellish the details. It was during the ten and one-half years we spent at the Mission that we grew to understand how God might use us. Julie is one way God has shown me what it means to be truly loved by another human being and I can't begin to thank her enough for agreeing to be my wife.

I also want to thank Pat Mentzer, my office

manager at the church. She has read each story and encouraged me to keep writing. I'm grateful, too, for Glenn Walkup's valuable assistance in formatting my text. He is a computer whiz.

You always wonder if people will really want to read what you have written. I also question why people would keep coming back Sunday after Sunday to hear what I have to share. God is truly amazing in that He speaks through the likes of us. And a special thanks to the people of Windsor United Methodist Church for putting up with a pastor who does such weird stuff on Sunday mornings. You are great people and Julie and I love you dearly.

I also appreciate my children for allowing me the freedom to serve at the Mission. Their lives were changed by the men as well. My oldest daughter shared with me the other day one of her experiences. Jeni and Betsy were scooping the loop in downtown Des Moines one evening when a homeless man came up to them. He said, *"I know you. You are Chaplain Bob's daughter and you have no business being down here. Go home!"* Jeni did not know the man, but he knew us. The men watched out for our family in many ways. We became their family as well while they lived in Des Moines. Thank you for letting the men be a part of your lives and for welcoming them into your home through these stories.

Introduction: Meeting Chaplain Bob

I like to know a bit about authors when reading material they have written and also learning why they found it important to share their stories in a written format. In 1991, I was serving a church in the Des Moines area as an associate pastor. The church was going through a rather difficult time and I had found myself drawn into the middle of the conflict. The really difficult part for me was that I valued people on both sides of the conflict, but due to my sense of loyalty I chose to protect the institution. Looking back now, it would have been better had I made the decision to be in ministry rather than listening to the voices that called me to take an administrative leadership position.

A good friend of mine, Jerry Ulin, who also happened to be a United Methodist pastor, heard much of my struggles and my complaining. Jerry had been serving downtown as the Skywalk Chaplain at the time. He had some really difficult health issues that were forcing him to take early retirement . I happened to be headed to Estes Park, Colorado, for a week at the YMCA of the Rockies camp. I knew Jerry had access to a cabin nearby and invited him to ride along with me, so he and his wife, Judy, took me up on the offer. While traveling, we spent a lot of time talking about what both of us were going to do in the coming year. Jerry suggested I might apply for the position of Skywalk Chaplain. The chaplaincy had recently become affiliated with the Door of Faith Mission as an outreach to the homeless who spent a lot of the day hanging out in the skywalk system.

It was an interesting suggestion but my practical side was having a really tough time with what that would

1

involve in my life. I considered the following:
>*There would be a really drastic reduction in
>salary.
>*Even worse, I would be giving up two weeks of
>vacation.
>*I doubted the position would last for more than a
>year due to some budget issues they were facing at
>the time.
>*I had no experience whatsoever working with
>homeless individuals, nor did I have any knowledge
>of what their problems were other than they had no
>place to live. (My only experience of the homeless
>had been the previous summer watching a man eat
>his lunch out of a garbage can in San Francisco
>when we had been on vacation. I still recall that I
>thought I would be sick to my stomach as I
>watched him. I stood by, though, and out of fear
>did nothing to provide food for him).

During this Colorado vacation, I took off one day and hiked into the mountains alone in an attempt to seek direction from God as to my future. It seemed from the Biblical record that at times others had gone to the mountains to hear a word from God. As I hiked, I noticed a river flowing toward the valley. I headed off toward the water, anticipating sitting there to think and be alone. As I approached, I noticed there was quite a bit of water flowing that day, but there were also rocks in the river bed which made it possible for one to walk up the river by jumping from stone to stone.

I started making my way up the stream and enjoying the experience of the day. At some point I thought that if I could walk up a river without getting wet, maybe I could do ministry and not be in a local church. I spent quite a bit of time that day alone with God. I remember calling Julie and telling her that I thought maybe

2

it was time to leave the ministry of the church and do something different. I would visit with Jerry on the way home and see if I had his blessing in applying for the position he had created a few years earlier.

In some ways my inexperience was a blessing. I did not have a lot of preconceived ideas that would get in the way of my learning what God was to require of me. My seminary experience at the University of Dubuque also would prove to be a blessing. I had attended a Presbyterian institution, but lived in a Catholic facility. The University had an agreement where students of three seminaries (also included was a Lutheran school) could take classes from any school and apply the credits earned toward graduation. These classes would be a great help to me as I found myself dealing with people of faith from many different traditions.

Over the course of the next ten and one-half years, our family would become family for many of the men who passed through the Mission. Occasionally, some of the men would come to stay at our home over the weekend. They would touch the lives of our children as well as Julie and me. Those years at the Mission would force us to move way beyond our comfort level. God truly has great things in store for each of us if we can walk by faith in the Lord.

Will the Real Chaplain Please Stand Up?

One of the aspects of my job over those ten-plus years at the Door of Faith Mission was the raising of issues surrounding homelessness. There were so many myths about the problem and how people view those caught in that condition. I once heard homelessness described as those caught up in hopelessness. That seemed to be one item that almost everybody had in common when they came through the front door seeking a place to live or some form of assistance. They had given up on themselves and their abilities.

I also came to see that most of their family and friends had given up on them as well. A family, in order to survive, had written the person off and had gone on with life in many cases as if the person had died. So I always enjoyed the opportunities to speak to different groups and organizations about the Mission and what we saw happening there in the lives of those God called us to serve. Several of those speaking engagements stand out in my memory and I would like to share one such experience with you.

A friend of mine, who also happens to be a United Methodist pastor, called one afternoon and invited me to speak at their Wednesday evening program. As we visited, he raised some concerns as to what the program might entail. His vision was to challenge the members of his church about the way they viewed both homelessness and how they reached out to serve those in need in their community. I suggested that maybe we could have one of the men dress up as the chaplain, pretend to be me, while I dressed in attire more representative of one of the men at

4

the Mission. It was agreed that at the end of the service I would then step up and reveal the switch and make a few closing comments about observations I had during the evening.

I had asked a man about my age, named Brian, to play my part, which he was more than willing to do. He had worked as a Mission deskman for quite a long time. The deskmen are the ones you meet when entering the building. They control the security of the Mission. It is also their job to get the individual to the right staff person when one needs assistance. At night, when the staff is gone, it was their job to make decisions that pertained to the well-being of the facility. Brian was good at the job and had a strong working knowledge of what happened at our building. He seemed to be a natural for the presentation that evening in that he would be able to answer any and all questions people would raise.

The Tuesday before we were to go that Wednesday, I received a call that a friend of ours was in trouble. He had lived for years at the Mission before moving out to an apartment. He had been on his own for around six months but had begun drinking again. If you have been drinking, you are not allowed to check into the Mission. Julie and I had made the decision to have him stay at our home until he was sober and able to return.

I was not comfortable with his being alone at our country home that night with Julie, so I told him he had to go with us to the church. He would be able to share or not share as he saw fit, but he would have to go with me. So that Wednesday afternoon, we drove north of Des Moines some 45 miles to speak at the church. Both of the men were a little bit nervous, but their greatest concern seemed to be whether they would have time for a cigarette break sometime in the evening.

We arrived and were greeted by the pastor. Brian

introduced himself as Chaplain Bob to Rev. Don, and I, along with my friend, introduced ourselves using the names Richard and Brian. The church had an evening meal for all on Wednesdays so we were invited to eat dinner with the members of the church. An interesting thing began to happen as soon as we entered the building. People came up and started talking with the person they assumed to be Chaplain Bob. After all, he was dressed in a sports coat and clearly looked the part of a chaplain. People studied the other two men he had brought along to show them what homeless men looked like. As we ate that evening, the only people who would speak with Richard and me were the children. They did not know better than to talk to the homeless, or at least they were not so nervous about our presence. This had been the first time I had noticed or felt what it would be like to have people assume I was a homeless man and it would have a lasting effect on me.

I have a bit of a dry sense of humor. So knowing we were about ready to go upstairs for the evening program, I asked Brian, who was playing Chaplain Bob, if Richard and I could go outside for a walk around the block so we might smoke before going upstairs. I knew Richard and Brian were dying for a smoke. Brian offered to go with us so he could smoke but I assured him that the two of us wanted to be alone for few moments to collect our thoughts before sharing upstairs. Besides, he needed to stay and visit with the church members and the pastor.

So Richard and I went outside, leaving Brian behind to suffer from nicotine withdrawal. He gave us a funny look as we left him and headed outside. I also wanted a few moments with Richard to assure him he did not have to speak that night. He was really shaky, yet looked the part of a person just off the street. We had dressed somewhat like homeless street people, and I had put on blue jeans and a tee shirt to make people think I, too, was homeless.

When dinner was completed, and Richard had finished smoking, we went upstairs. Brian did his introduction and showed a short video. He then took questions that people had about the Mission and did a wonderful job sharing what happens there. He really enjoyed the evening, not only in seeing how people were fooled by their impressions of the homeless, but I also believe he was clinging to the hope that he could one day rise to a position where people would again value him. Richard got up and shared what had been going on in his life and how he had been drinking up until the past day or so. He had never been really sure of himself but he did a great job.

It was then my turn to rise and share a bit about myself, all of which is true.

I told them I had been divorced in February of 1985.

I shared that I had three children and told a little bit about each of them and how they were doing in school.

I also related to them that I had not had a drink since April of 1988. (I often wondered if I was an alcoholic or merely chose to be drunk at times so as to avoid my problems. Some things had happened in my life that spring that caused me to choose to never again use alcohol, which is the number one drug in the United States).

I said that I had remarried in June of 1987 and that my wife was a teacher.

It was at that point I stated, "*By the way, I am the real Chaplain Bob. I work at the Door of Faith Mission.*" I then asked them a question: "*Why is it that since we came to your church that no one has talked to us, other than your pastor and the children?*" I also said that I had observed how they all wanted to speak to whom they thought was the real Chaplain. There was a strange silence that settled over the listeners at that point. We concluded the service and were invited to the back of the church to greet folks as they left, and to visit with any who wanted to share.

A strange thing happened. I might add it's not what I had hoped would happen.

People came up and wanted to visit with me. They completely ignored the other two men who they now understood were homeless. I also was never invited to return to the church to speak again. I suspect the pastor fulfilled his purpose of raising not only awareness about homelessness, but also in lifting up some stereotypes that many in the congregation wished could remain buried.

But the evening had a dramatic effect on me that I had not anticipated. God seemed to break through to me that night. I would never again be able to share quite the same way with groups when I went out to speak. I had often invited men to go with me to tell their stories. Those stories often were the most inspiring of anything I had to offer. But it hit me that night that in some ways I had been putting them on display for the purpose of the Mission, at a terrible cost to them. I had been so engrossed in talking with people I had never noticed how the men had been treated at the time. (Many times they were offered love at other churches, but the nagging question still remained with me that I might have been using them to push the Mission's agenda).

I started encouraging them to avoid publicity when invited to share their stories through the Mission newsletter. I still allowed them to go with me if they chose but it was with a completely different mind-set and I made sure they were included in conversations. Effort was made on my part to be aware of their feelings and how they were handling the situation and people's comments. When somebody in the audience made assertions or statements that bordered on the judgmental, I would redirect the conversation to bring out the great things the man had done to get to the point where he was now.

I also have to admit that we adapted this presentation into a "What's My Line?" format and allowed the church groups and schools to guess at the end who was the chaplain by our answers. They never picked me as the chaplain. It had occurred to me that we have misconceptions about those different from us in society. I really loved the time spent at the Mission and the educational part of the position. You see, I came to understand that God had set me aside for ten and one-half years of further study before allowing me to return to a local congregation to share what I had learned about myself and my relationship with the Living God.

Being unwanted, unloved, uncared for, forgotten by everybody, I think that is a much greater hunger, a much greater poverty than the person who has nothing to eat.   *-Mother Teresa*

My Teacher

There are people who God causes to enter our lives. I can think of four or five such persons who have so affected my life and values system that without their presence, I would not be the person I am today. How can one even begin to thank them for what they have given to us? Maybe by being a better person and working to make their lessons a way of life. One such man crossed my path during the ten and one-half years I worked for the Door of Faith Mission.

He appeared at the Mission like most of the men. His apparent need was for a place to stay. It was obvious from the first contact with Sam, though, that he was not like the rest of the men who lived there. Sam was thoughtful and so gentle in both conversation and deed. He was highly intelligent and spoke with such clarity that it was apparent he had been in high positions at some point in his life. I never once heard him raise his voice to another human being or even remotely mistreat another person in the whole time I knew him. His health was not good, but no one knew the exact extent of that until it was too late.

Sam was offered a grant position for which he received free room and board along with $40.00 a week. His grant job was being the morning deskman, a position he dearly loved. (He would eventually get crosswise with another staff person who was in charge of the grant jobs and was forced to work in the outlet store).

Sam was a black man. I would later come to know that at one point in his life he had served in one of the 50 states under the governor as Secretary relating to race relations for that particular state. During our conversations it became apparent to him that I did not have a very good grasp of what it would be like to have been born Afro-

American. He offered one day to help educate me. (I mean that in the kindest sense of the word; Sam became my teacher). During those few years he stayed at the Mission we became good friends. I have suspicions why he came to live there, but it was not due to any addiction. His ex-wife would later tell me that in all the things he had ever done in his life, those years at Mission were the best of his life. It was here in Des Moines that Sam would find a way to love and serve those most in need of a kind word and a generous heart.

It was also during those years that I came to have an understanding of how people from different cultures experience life and insults at the hands of those who are not evil, but possibly just a bit ignorant. I am sure as we talked Sam must have suffered by some of the questions and comments I made to him. And yet he patiently shared and conversed with me over the years, helping me understand things I had little knowledge about. (Growing up in rural Iowa doesn't afford one much opportunity to experience the world) .

I got a call one day from the outlet store. It was Sam. He said, *"Bob, there are some really nice suits that have been donated and you would look great in them, I think you should come over here."* Sam was a great dresser and he took me on as his project. He was right. The suits fit and for a small fee at the tailor shop and the dry cleaners, I had a pair of $500.00 suits. He was always looking out for others.

Sam had a night job at an expensive restaurant doing dishes. He did not need the money but his son was in prison and he was working to provide needed items for him while in prison and also upon his release from prison. Even though his health was quickly deteriorating, Sam continued to worry about others rather than himself. I did not realize how sick he was, for he chose to not tell anyone about his own health needs. The outlet store was not air conditioned and the heat was unbearable that summer. I remember coming to work one morning and being informed that Sam had passed away the night before in the hospital.

The owner of the restaurant was notified of Sam's death. His response was to request how much money was needed for the funeral and he would help to pay for the expenses. It did not matter where Sam was; he connected with folks and quickly became their friend. His ex-wife helped to make funeral arrangements. She informed me that Sam would have wanted me to do the service. I remember that day as if it were yesterday. One time Sam had been on a three-day religious retreat and loved some of the music, so we asked other guys to come and sing one of the songs from that weekend. Different people got up to share how he had impacted their lives. His son was there for the funeral. (Unfortunately the prison system required him to be in chains even though he was soon to be released).

Sam was but one example of those individuals who would touch not only my life but the life of my family. My wife and children still have a special place in their hearts for him and the love he shared with us. I have been humbled to realize what Christian faith abounded at the Mission. I am more humbled to realize that the expression of that faith was at times more evident in the men who lived there than the staff who worked there. It was through such examples as Sam that I came to know what it means to live the Christian life. Too bad that seminary training can't instill that in the pastors they train.

In your own life, I would like to invite you to put this book down. To recall some of the people God has brought across your path to help grow your Christian faith. If they are still alive, take a moment and either call them or drop them a letter thanking them for their impact upon your spiritual development. I also would encourage you to invite God to perform a work in your life so that some day another person may tell this story, using your name as the one God called to teach them of the love manifested in Jesus Christ.

Thank you, Sam, for the gift you gave me. I really did come to love you and to understand God's calling in my life in a new and vital way due in large part to people like you. I pray you have found the peace you searched for all of your life.

Do all the good you can, by all the means you can, in all the ways you can, in all the places you can, at all the times you can, to all the people you can, as long as ever you can.   *-John Wesley*

I'm Sorry You Didn't Stop

Do you ever have regrets? Let me share with you a letter written in 1985.

Dear Harold (not his real name),
I am glad your letter got here. I am sorry you didn't stop here. It is difficult for me to tell you I am getting some help from Mary _____. Enclosed is as I say some money for you and use it wisely. You should have stopped here to see me. I am not working and my income isn't the best. I am glad to help you as much as I can. I wish you could come back even if you think its not the best. If you want to stay out there I will help all I can. Mary is help me as I am to old to work. This is Saturday evening and I just got the mail. Please take care of the money as I don't know when I can send any more and Mary is helping me and she will be glad & surprised to know you wrote at last.
PLEASE WRITE: I hope to get some stamps to send you. I been planning on going in a home where I can live and give up the apartment. Mary is helping me she is real good. The rent on the apartment is paid for this month. I will try to get this in the mail on Sunday. You can call me here anytime for a short time.
                                    With Love Mother
I'll send you more money on Sunday or Monday

            Harold _____
            U.S. Post Office
            General Delivery
            Omaha, NE.

The letter was addressed with his name on the

envelope. The year I came across the letter was 1998, some 13 years after it had been written to her son. I am not sure about you but I can hear my parents telling me goodbye every time I re-read that letter. In their words are the emotions of love built up over the years since my birth. Mom also feels a need to share something with me to make my life a bit easier. (I have noticed that with my own children, I always pick up the tab at the restaurant, offer to provide something I think they might want, or seek to find some way of letting them know how much I love them). A parent's love is something that never ceases regardless of the life their child is living or may have lived.

This mom was saddened her son had been in town and not stopped by to see her but had at least written her a note to which she could respond. She did not have his address but realized he was living in Omaha and so she took a chance of having the letter delivered by the Post Office.

Later, Harold came to Des Moines and stayed at the Mission. One Wednesday I came to work and the man at the desk informed me that Harold was not looking at all well. He thought maybe I should go in and see if he would go to the hospital. I still remember sitting on the bottom bunk across from his bed. There were about four feet of space between the beds in the dorm, and absolutely no privacy. Harold was not able to sit up but he was still speaking and he flatly refused to go to the hospital. I made a mental note that he had been spitting on the floor beside his bed but it did not occur to me how sick he was at the time.

The next day when I came to work, I was notified that they had called an ambulance and sent him to the hospital. Broadlawns Hospital had decided he was much too sick for them to treat and he was rushed to the University of Iowa Hospital. We were notified on Friday that he had died from a number of serious health problems. The hospital social worker was looking for next of kin. In checking his admittance card, we found he had listed no family or phone numbers in case of an emergency. I asked the hospital what they would do with the ashes? They would hold them for a while and then dispose of them. So we asked if they would return them and his things to the Mission and we would find a way to bury the ashes.

A few days later a package arrived at the Mission. Inside, two plastic bags held all his earthly belongings: The clothes he was wearing at the time along with his billfold. The billfold contained around $150.00 in cash. In the meantime, his paycheck had come to the Mission in the amount of $300.00. Here was the sum total of his life:

A bag of old clothing
$450.00
An envelope
A few things in his locker in the dormitory.

Of special interest was the above letter from his mother, which was in the envelope. It was yellowed from years of travel, not to mention the creases from being folded and unfolded as it was read over and over. On the yellow paper were stains that appeared to be from tears. He had carried that letter for some years, the only reminder of a mother's love. I have every reason to believe that was the last contact they had with each other, in that we found no other letters in his belongings. We searched the internet to find relatives that related to his birth certificate, but were unsuccessful.

Over the years I have had families call me to find the whereabouts of loved ones. I can only imagine the pain this mom carried as she worried for a son she had lost touch with for so many years. That kind of grief is not something a parent ever learns to deal with in life

I made a decision a few months later that the secretary of the Mission helped carry out. That decision was probably not completely legal, but I believe "Permission is much harder to get than forgiveness". We cashed his check, took the other money and I went to the Winterset Monument Company on University Avenue in Des Moines to see what a tombstone would cost. They agreed to provide a granite stone for the $450.00 we had if we would pay the tax. I then contacted a friend who ran a county home and asked if we could bury Harold in the cemetery. (That cemetery would become the final resting place of others in future years). I had dug graves for years as a means of paying for my education so it was not a difficult task to bury the remains.

The more difficult item was the setting of a stone. I had little skill in such a task, but proceeded with good intentions. When the task was finished and I stood in that cemetery where the grass was higher than my waist, I felt a flood of sadness sweep over me. It was certainly a peaceful spot with a small farm pond nearby. The cattle from the county home would come up to the fence and were curious about my truck parked outside the cemetery gate. But it hit me that day how alone people are in this world, and how far we can travel from those who truly love us due to our addictions. Harold was to be soon forgotten by the world, but he will never be forgotten by me. His brothers and sisters may have written him off for his lifestyle of drinking, but God is always looking out for us to return to our senses, as in the story of the Prodigal Son.

I realized somewhere along the way at the Mission that most of the men who came through those doors would end up dying from the disease of alcoholism. But I also made a commitment that while they were there and sober, I wanted them to know the love of God and that I would try to faithfully live that out to them. God did not create us to be alone. Sometimes the only one there to share a life with another person may be _____(fill in your name). Will you be God's hands and feet reaching out to a hurting world?

What we have done for ourselves alone dies with us; what we have done for others and the world, remains and is immortal.
-Albert Pike

Which One Will Make It?

There are times when events happen that change the whole course of your life. I have found more often than not that we don't realize how dramatically that change will affect us until years later.

We just finished having dinner with a young pastor and his family on a recent Sunday after returning home from morning worship. We had received a call that they were on vacation and stopping in Des Moines and wondered if there was some time to get together with Julie and me. It had been a busy a week for both our families, so we decided that lunch after church was the only time we had available. So, as Paul Harvey so often said, "*And now the rest of the story.*"

More than ten years ago I was sitting in my office when the deskman called to inform me there were two young men in the outer office and they wanted to check into the Door of Faith Mission. Could I possibly do the intake interview with both of them? We usually met individually with the men but since they had come together as a pair, I invited both of them to come in at the same time. They were young, both just barely 18 years of age. They came to Des Moines from an eastern state because at the previous mission they had heard of our Mission in Des Moines. Word there was that it was a great working man's Mission. You could be sure of work going out of the Mission each day, where you get some money in your pocket while figuring out what you wanted from life. So here they sat in my office with the world under their belt, knowing all the answers but few of the questions. It was a really simple interview and no reason not to accept both the men. The Mission had 78 beds available and that day we happened to have several open spots, which was not often

27

the case back in those days. I remember looking at them and making the snap judgment that one would surely succeed and the other would soon be gone, judging from the way they answered the intake questions.

It was hardly a week later and the one young man was gone from the Mission, that being the one I was sure would be successful. The other young man was still there and doing fairly well. I'm going to call him Joe (which is not his real name), and we had started to become friends. What is more, my wife, Julie, was starting to take him under her wing as a mother might do. You see, we came to hear his story. He had been 14 years old when his mother developed cancer. He was 16 years of age when she died, and he found himself living alone. He did have a dad, but the father had many problems, including alcohol dependency. So Joe found himself working, attending school and living with whomever he could for those last couple years of high school. He was clearly bright and had done well in school, considering all that he had endured.

His mom's family was somewhat put off with the father for all the years of drinking and Joe often found himself caught in the middle of those conflicts. He stayed for several months and then one day just disappeared. One of the difficult parts of my job was getting close to the guys and then having them just up and leave with no word or forwarding address. In this situation, it was even more difficult in that I had to tell Julie that night that he was gone and I doubted we would ever see him again. God, though, had other plans.

Another 6-12 months would pass and one day he returned to Des Moines and asked if he could check back into the Mission. Men were usually allowed two-three times at the Mission before it became difficult to re-enter. So Joe was re-admitted and seemed to pick up right where he had been before. Our relationship continued to grow and not always having the best professional distancing skills, I started to see him as a part of our family. He was growing in relationship to other staff at the Mission as well. He was put on the desk for a while as one of the deskmen. We had started conversation about college and what he would do when he finished school. Sometimes, though, jobs get in the way of long-term personal growth. Joe took an evening dishwashing job at a trendy restaurant in the Des Moines area and did such a great job that the owner offered him a full-time position. The owner had some other issues and I jumped to several conclusions when Joe left the mission a second time to live with the owner and keep the job. We did not see him after he left that night for work, and eventually he left town again without a word to any of us.

It would be close to a year when one Sunday morning Julie and I were at the Mission monitoring the Faith Café. (Faith Café was a free meal served every day of the week to anybody who needed a great meal. The serving time was from 10:50 a.m. -11:20 a.m., and then with clean-up, the mission was ready to serve lunch to the men who lived at the Mission.) It was during this time that Joe walked back into our lives. I remember Julie jumping up and running over to give him a hug. As I said, we had become emotionally over-extended with this young man. He was fast becoming a part of our family.

He again checked into the Mission. But this time several of the staff started to put pressure on him to make changes that would have consequences with how he lived his life. We wanted him to know our love existed for him regardless of what he did, but that we also had expectations of him as well. He checked into our local community college to see about grants and loans, etc. That in itself is a difficult process when you are homeless and don't have the needed W-2's and all the other material. He was accepted

and started classes. It was no surprise that he did
wonderfully in college and really started to shine in this
area of his life. He worked a bit both at the Mission and at
a grant job. (Grant jobs are given to the men so they room
and board for free and at the time they were given a $40.00
a week stipend to help with items. In return, they worked
some 24-30 hours a week doing jobs at the Mission.) But
we made it clear his real job was getting on with life.

Joe got a summer job working at a church related
institution. This experience, along with the wonderful care
he received there, would help solidify his desire to become
a minister. Each weekend Julie or I would pick him up and
he spent the weekends that summer at our home. In the
fall, he returned to the Mission to live in one of the halfway houses that the Mission maintained. During that year
we really got close. My job had changed and I was put in
charge of the houses. The men who lived there said I only
thought I was in charge, that they were the real leaders and
looking back that may be more true than I knew at the time.
That year was a wonderful experience with the seven to
eight guys who lived there. We had Sunday nights
together for house meetings and supper and then a short
Bible study. Joe's grades continued to improve with
mostly A's and a few B's sprinkled in each time the grades
came out.

He was growing and then God did something really
wonderful. A young woman came into his life and they
started to date. I cautioned him not to get too involved
with all the school ahead of him. But he was listening to
God more than I was. They were married in December
before Christmas. Looking back again, she has been the
best thing that could have ever happened in his life. The
best thing unless one considers the wonderful children they
have been given by God. This past year he graduated from
college with over a 3.5 grade point average.

Joe has been serving several churches for the past three years as their pastor. He and his family have been loved there and continue to thrive. He is moving to begin seminary, which will take another four years of school. God has provided another place for him to serve churches while he attends school and I believe he will continue to grow in his faith as he learns what God has in store for them in the coming years.

First impressions are exactly that: FIRST IMPRESSIONS. They often are what we base much of our assumptions upon and seldom do they reflect all that we need in making a decision. Unfortunately, we as individuals are sometimes slow to get over those first impressions as we give people a chance to grow and develop in their lives. This young man and his family have affected my wife and me more than any other relationship we have experienced through the Mission. It has been a blessing to be a small part of his life and to watch him develop under God's guidance.

He shared once a quote in a newsletter for the Mission. I don't know if the organization liked the quote or not, but I really thought it summed up the heart of why George H. started the mission years ago. Joe told folks that the Door of Faith was not responsible for his life and the direction it was going. Rather, the Mission merely provided a safe place where he, along with God, could figure things out and create a life that had meaning. What more can be said of us as Christians than that?

AT THE MISSION WE PROVIDED A PLACE WHERE IT IS SAFE FOR MEN TO GROW INTO THEIR PERSONAL FAITH WITH GOD. In our own churches we need to provide such places where people can experience God in their own time. That leaves the work of salvation up to God while we lend a helping hand. I and Julie hope to continue to be a part of his life and to be able

to lend a helping hand now and then when we are needed.
Joe knows, though, that I will have to be held in check
because sometimes I have a tendency to stick my nose in
and give advice that may not always be needed. I hope,
though, that my love for him outweighs anything else I may
have shared with him in the past. I consider him not only a
good friend but a son. (Joe is currently serving as a
minister and attending seminary).

I expect to pass through this world but once. Any good thing therefore that I can do, or any kindness that I can show a fellow being, let me do it now. Let me not defer or neglect it, for I shall not pass this way again.
*   - Stephen Grellet*

Pass the Bottle

Over the years that I served at the Door of Faith Mission, many different men would come and go in my life. Some would simply pass through Des Moines. Then there would be other men who would spend an extended part of their life here in the capital city of Iowa. I would know one such man during the final stages of his life. There is one fact that doesn't change: "*You drink long enough and you will die from alcohol.*" Wild Bill would be one such example of what alcoholism inflicts upon people. Not only does alcohol rob us of any productivity, it also destroys the physical bodies that God has given us to provide transportation of the soul. At times the soul is even compromised from long-term alcohol consumption.

Representatives from the Mission used to go out on the streets every Saturday night and distribute food to folks in need of a hot meal. Volunteer groups from local churches would go along and serve those meals. Many of the folks we met on a Saturday night would never come to the Mission to live, but they would receive services from us just the same. Wild Bill was one case in point. His life had become totally unmanageable due to the effects of alcohol. He was unable to face a day without being over the legal limit for intoxication. He would come to the Mission during the day for the free meal (called Faith Café) when he was sober enough. But we often saw him on the streets on Saturday night as we made the rounds with the free meals.

Bill had a disability check from the government. He had convinced the Social Security office that he was unable to work. In those early years, that was an easier process than it has become now to qualify as a disabled person. The check, though, did nothing to enhance the quality of his life. When he finally secured the disability status, he was awarded back pay from the point when he had first made application minus the medical expense that had been billed against the expected disability. This provided him a rather large sum of money. He quickly secured an apartment and began drinking. He also included many of his friends in the party. It does not take a man long to go through the excess money. It also doesn't take landlords long to realize they have a tenant who is a problem for them. So gradually many of the men would find their way to places of residence run by the slum landlords of Des Moines. These more often than not were really nasty apartments.

Bill had developed liver problems over the years, such as psoriasis of the liver. He also had developed hepatitis. The two diseases were ravaging his body and accelerating the destructive tendencies of the his alcoholism. Word came to the mission that Bill was in really tough shape and that the guys he was living with wanted us to come check on him. Another staff member and I went to the apartment that was on the Saturday Night Ministry Route, where we had been many times. There were six men living in the apartment, which was on the third floor of the building. We found Bill between the second and third floors, lying in the stairway. His eyes were completely yellow and he was non-responsive. The two of us carried him out of the building and put him in our van so we could get him to Broadlawns Hospital (this is the Polk County hospital, where they provide free care to individuals of the county who do not have health insurance). He was to live several days in the hospital before death would overtake him. Bill never regained consciousness after arriving at the hospital.

When death happens to men living on the street, their bodies are cremated as the cheapest way of disposing

36

of the body. If they happen to have living relatives who will step forward, they can receive the ashes. Many families, though, are somewhat reluctant to accept the ashes for fear they will also have to pay any outstanding funeral expenses.

We talked one day in staff and thought we should have a memorial service for Bill. We did not expect many of his friends to come but felt it was important for those of us who knew him to take a moment to reflect on his life. The day was selected for the service. The time was set right after lunch, expecting more people to come at that time. There were about eight of us who gathered that day. I shared some opening comments from the funeral ritual. I read some scripture. And then I offered prayer. It was at this point in time we invited those present to share comments of Bill if they wished. Several staff reflected briefly on Bill and his life, before one of the men who was living with him on the street offered the following comments. I have long since forgotten the name of the man who shared these words, but I remember the eulogy.

"Bill was a great guy. He was a true friend. You could trust him. An example of that trust: When we would be sitting around a campfire drinking, Bill would always pass the bottle the same direction around the circle to make sure we all got a fair amount of alcohol when our turn came."

I could not help but find myself being taken aback a bit by that eulogy. It was certainly a comment I had not heard before when presiding over a funeral. I shared with Julie, my wife, that night, *"I really hope when I die that folks can share more about me than I was honest and always passed the bottle the same way around the circle when we were getting drunk."* But as the days wore on into months, those words kept coming back to me and I began to see them in a different light. What more could have

37

been said about Bill to show his honesty than the fact that he shared his alcohol equally with his friends.

If you know anything about alcoholism, you know that alcohol has become their God. Nothing else matters in life more than having enough to keep you drunk. And yet here was a man whose total life had been destroyed by his consumption of this drug and yet his honesty still remained. He was not a thief. He cared about his friends. And regardless of how much he needed a drink, he still shared with those who had needs as desperate as his own. That was the man I had come to know over the years. He was honest. He cared for people. It just so happened he was drunk all the time.

That service got me to thinking about my own life: What will people say about me when I am gone? Will I be missed?

Will the way I have lived my life be an inspiration or a sense of embarrassment?

And how about you? What do you think people will say when you are gone?

"YES, HE ALWAYS PASSED THE BOTTLE THE SAME WAY!"

What is success in life? .... To leave this world a bit better, whether by a healthy child, a garden patch or a redeemed social condition....To know even one life has breathed easier because you have lived....this is to have succeeded.
*   -Ralph Waldo Emerson*

Waking Up in My Right Mind

I shared an office with Brother Patrick for a little over one year. During that time we became close friends and had more than just a professional relationship. One of his comments has stayed with me throughout the years. A quote from one of the ancient Monks, *"I thank God each morning that I wake up in my right mind."* Mental illness was an issue in many of the men's lives. Depression seemed to be a constant problem that often led to relapse a few months after they gave up alcohol or drugs. There were, though, men who experienced mental illness that went far beyond a situational or seasonal depression diagnosis.

I had been told in seminary that most of the people who came to our office could benefit from a caring, listening pastor as they worked through their difficulties. But the same professor also cautioned us that there was that 5% we would encounter who needed serious professional counseling. I am not sure what percentage of men we encountered at the Door of Faith Mission needed long term counseling, but I suspect it was greater than 5% of the population. We in this country have done a great disservice to them when we released them to the streets in their own care. I suspect many of the men would have benefitted from a combination of drug therapy and counseling. The sad fact, though, was that due to limited health care dollars, that type of care was often not available to the extent it was needed. Let me share several stories to give you a flavor of the issue.

I found myself sitting across from a young man I will call Glen. As he pleaded his case for admittance to the

Mission, it became apparent he had some needs that far exceeded the scope of what we could offer. But it was also equally clear that he was better off residing at the Mission than living on the streets. It was decided we would accept him into the program and attempt to secure psychological treatment for him. One difficulty would also become clear to me shortly after starting to work at the Mission. That was that many of the men did not feel they had a problem that required counseling. They often refused to accept assistance. If they did receive counseling, they often refused to continue the medication prescribed for their specific disease.

As Glen and I visited, he would break into laughter at different comments I made. I began to notice him looking off into the distance and it appeared he was visiting with someone else in the room. Eventually I asked him, "Whom are you speaking to?" *"Bob, don't you see the angel in the room, after all you are the pastor here?"* I remember thinking after he left the room, what if there really was an angel in the room and he saw things in the spiritual realm that I was not able to see. I know the medical diagnosis for his condition, but I still could not help but wonder if certain people see things the rest of us don't. I also wondered about some of the old Biblical accounts where Jesus confronted those today we would call mentally ill and offered healing to them.

Glen would eventually find his way to the kitchen where he cooked breakfast. I was told by several of the men that we had to do something to help him. That morning he was in the kitchen with rolled up tin foil stuffed in his ears and nostrils to prevent the radio waves from bouncing off the old KRNT radio tower. He claimed the aliens were trying to take over his brain and he was only protecting himself from their attempts to transmit messages to his head.

He would eventually become so delusional that he chose to leave the Mission. He had become so offended by the politicians in Washington that he felt it his task to go straighten them out. He informed us we would need a new breakfast cook and that he was on his way to fix things out east. I kept watching over the next few months on the evening news to see if he would be arrested and show up on the 6:00 o'clock news.

How do you help someone who is so convinced by the voices? It is no wonder that people roam around the country when they are at the mercy of such illnesses.

A second man comes to mind who had similar delusions, only his were of the religious nature. He too had a lot in common with Glen. Both of the these men were great workers. They were caring in their own ways. It was also apparent although they heard different voices, that both equally believed they were special and chosen to carry out certain tasks. I will call this second individual Bob. He had the belief that he was a messenger sent from God to warn the world about sin. He message was very simple. Bob always stuck his finger in your face and shouted, "*REPENT*!" He clearly understood himself to be the modern-day John the Baptist sent to prepare the way for Jesus' return. He lived a life that was somewhat similar to the Biblical account of John as related in the Gospels.

I remember seeing him walking back from Quick Trip one night when I was going home and I stopped to pick him up and offered him a ride back to the Mission. He began to preach to me the moment he entered the car. I found myself contemplating what the masses must have thought when John came into the wilderness and began preaching. What must the religious leaders have thought when he called them the names he did and warned people to flee the snakes. It really gave me a whole new understanding of John's message when Bob began to preach against me that night. I am not sure what I had done to set him off but the message came out directed to me and those in the churches of the day.

Bob was out of control that evening, as his mental illness caused him to unleash the words of warning directed toward me. I have to admit I was also a bit taken aback and found myself that night speaking to Julie about the incident and wondering about things I did daily and what God really thought about me as well. Is that not the place of a prophet? They speak so the rest of us will look at our lives and repent. Was he delusional or a messenger sent from God? That is the hard thing about mental illness; it looks at times like reality as they seek to draw us into their world.

Bob would eventually leave the Mission. In his locker he left behind tools valued at over a thousand dollars. We also found the Gospel according to Bob. In it was some forty pages of warnings to the world about the impending doom God was about to release upon the world. It was written in much the same vein as the Book of Revelation, as he worked through each of the dooms about to be set upon the earth. The staff visited a bit about the writings and assumed Bob had fled to the hills to hide out as he awaited the destruction about to be unleashed on the world. He never returned nor did we ever hear of him again.

Pain is not always physical.

What a blessing it is to wake up in the morning and be in our right mind.

God, how can we love and assist those who suffer in the world today?

What words can we speak that will provide some assurance to them that they are loved and accepted?

God, could it possibly be that through folks like this you still speak to us, calling us to repentance, even if they are delusional? .

44

God, give me understanding for those who suffer on a daily basis.

Verily, when the day of judgment comes, we shall not be asked what we have read, but what we have done.   *-Thomas A Kempis*

Food Is the Way to Man's Heart

      One of most anticipated times at the Door of Faith Mission was mealtime. Equally true is that this was also one of the most unhappy times, depending upon who happened to be the cook at a given period during the year. Several of the men would work in the kitchen on grant job status. (That means when they worked 30 hours a week, they got room and board free, and a $40.00 grant to help with other expenses they might have).

      The Mission, during the first nine or so years I worked there, made a real commitment to the meals served, understanding that we valued the men by the quality of food we provided. Scott Larsen also believed strongly, as did previous directors, that we should serve nothing to the men we would not be excited to eat as well. In turn, the Mission spent a fairly sizable amount of money on purchasing food from different vendors along with ordering from the Food Bank of Central Iowa. We also found that donations would come in from individuals and companies that helped to supplement the food we served.

      The cooks were busy in those early years I was at the Mission. At breakfast, you could expect up to 50 men between 6:00 a.m. - 6:30 a.m. Faith Café was served to non-residents from 10:50 a.m. - 11:20 a.m., with an expected number of people in the 80-100 range. Lunch for the residents and staff was from Noon to 12:30 p.m. and normally there would be 30-40 at this meal. Supper was served from 5:30 p.m - 6:00 p.m. and the numbers would run from 50-60. The kitchen also had to prepare some 30 sack lunches for those men out working each day. On

49

Saturday night they would send out on the streets between 300 - 400 meals that were distributed around the city.

We had one cook who was at the Mission different times during the 10 ½ years I served there as Chaplain, who could have cooked at most of the restaurants in Des Moines. In fact, when he was cooking, the meals were usually better than the surrounding restaurants. He cared for the guys who came through the lines for meals and this was the way he showed that concern for them.

I remember one Sunday in December receiving a call from a man who had been deer hunting and he wondered if we would like to have deer donated to the Mission. It appears his hunting party had shot a doe and no one had any interest in cleaning and paying for the processing fee, so they were looking for a place to get rid of it. We often had wild game donated, but usually it was wrapped in freezer paper and dropped off during the year when people cleaned out the freezers in their basements.

I called up and asked our cook, Jim, wondering if he would have any interest in the deer. I was told to have them pull around back and we would take care of it. They dropped off the deer and we loaded it on an old lift that ran from the ground up the back of the building to the kitchen. I helped him drag it into the Mission and we put it in the cooler. Jim assured me that after people went to bed, he would skin it, butcher it and then freeze it.

The next day, when I came to work, I was told the task was finished and that some Tuesday we would have a wild-game meal. A few months later we were treated to the most wonderful experience of deer steaks, pheasant and other types of wild game that had been left for the men. Unfortunately, around the Mission word often got out to the administration. I remember Scott asking about the deer one day and so I related the story. He had some real concerns about the health department finding out and stated that would be the last time we would do such a stunt. Then Scott commented, *"Or at least that is the last time I want to hear of such a thing happening."* Scott's heart went out to the men and rules were meant for serving them, not for preventing us from doing ministry. I learned what it meant to ask for forgiveness rather than permission. He once told me that if it helped the men, to do it, and then we would worry about what we had done. There would be times I found myself in interesting situations because of that practice, but I never was able to stop the practice.

This excellent cook unfortunately would come and go from the Mission as the seasons of the year changed. You could be sure that five months or so in the summer he would not be cooking. During those times he would be outside camping. (Camping means living in the woods on your own where there are no rules and one can do what he likes). The first time I met him was when I wandered into his camp off Ingersoll Avenue in Des Moines, along with Scott, who was showing me some of the camps. I remember walking around back and seeing these two men there and having Jim yell as us that it was a stupid thing to walk into a camp and not let the men know you were coming. Jim told us, *"You two idiots could get yourself killed doing that."* That would be a lesson I learned and from then on I always yelled out, *"It's Bob from the Door of Faith Mission."* I wasn't sure they would not hurt me, but I knew if they did they would be banned from the Mission for meals and that was a price most of them would not be willing to pay.

We were looking for camps one day behind the Governor's mansion. That was a place where four-six camps were normally found, one of them being more like a small home dug out in the hillside. I remember one of the guys being slightly drunk and a bit angry telling us that if we wanted to help them we would bring them

Thanksgiving dinner to their camp. It was late October when we had made the call, and I made a mental note that we would deliver a turkey there on Thanksgiving Day. When we had finished serving some 300 plus meals that coming Thanksgiving Day, I went to the camp with another person and we delivered the dinner. The man was somewhat shocked to think we would do that, but he also accepted the gift. I understood that it was a small thing to extend a common act of hospitality and those acts often paid off in the future as I was given the chance to work with different individuals.

Over the years, Jim and I have kept in close contact. Some four years now out of the Mission, he is one of the men who still calls to check in, or to ask for my assistance when he or another of the men we knew is in trouble. I was able to give him a special gift recently, "A Study Bible". We have talked about faith and he has been reading a lot of Julie's books on angels. I am amazed how God works through small acts of kindness we sow and years later allow us to be the living Christ for others who are seeking a spiritual encounter with God.

This same cook has offered Julie cooking lessons over the years. After one such class he gave her a new chef's coat and white hat so she could look the part even if she did not meet his standards in the culinary field. The problem with his personal cook book is that it is based on 80 servings, so we have to break it down a bit for our family use. He knew my favorites were fudge, cheese cake and pie. I could be expected to add a good 20 pounds during the winter when he was the cook. He had the same effect on most of the staff at the Mission.

I believe we all have gifts.

I believe God wants us to use those gifts to serve others and to help them enter into a relationship with God together with us. How do you use the gifts God has given you?

It is one of the most beautiful compensations of this life that no man can sincerely try to help another without helping himself.
                    -Ralph Waldo Emerson

Sign, Sign, Everywhere a Sign

I have heard the old saying that we do what we have to do in order to get by in life. Probably nowhere else in society is that more true than as it relates to those who find themselves homeless and trying to exist on the streets. There are a number of reasons surrounding their current predicament which has forced them into shelters or making the choice to try and exist outside on the streets. Different organizations and church affiliated groups have tried to name those reasons:

Drugs
Alcohol
Mental illness
Lack of motivation
Sin

I soon found that it really did not matter so much *why* they were in their particular situations. What does matter is that we are called to minister unto them in the Name of Christ.

Mother Teresa replied when asked if she ever got discouraged, *"I was not called to a ministry of success but rather to a ministry of compassion."* Her well-being did not depend upon her success of failure. Her life depended upon how she responded to the call of Christ in her life. Somewhere along the way I learned that the majority of the people would not be able to make the needed changes that would allow them to live lives the way we believed life should be lived. I also came to understand that for those who found the way out, it could be directly related to God. At some point in their life they needed to hear, as we need to hear the message, that God loves us and cares for us unconditionally. If people are to hear that then we are going to have to step up and be the messenger.

What I saw instead was how humiliating life had

become for many on the streets. One example: People holding signs begging for money at stop signs as cars passed. Can you imagine what it does to your self respect to sit on a street corner and beg for money? The first time I saw such begging was in Mexico, when we were on a mission trip with Borne Again Ministries out of Adel, Iowa. I still recall those images of parents sitting on the side-walk while they sent their children after the Americans asking for a quarter. It is amazing to me that in a country as wealthy as America we also have the same type of poverty which forces persons to beg for money.

I also would admit that I was surprised at how much money comes in to those who can give away their self respect in order to continue living. I know there are critics who will say they should get their life in order and I am not opposed to that suggestion. I am not sure how I would live if I lost all my wealth and was forced to live on the street. I was told years ago at the Door of Faith Mission by a man named Steve that on a good day signing (holding a sign out by Valley West Mall) he might get $100.00. I seriously doubt that with all the publicity from different missions in Des Moines discouraging giving money to people, that you could accumulate that much in a day any longer.

I have read the signs:

I WILL WORK FOR FOOD.

EX-VETERAN, DOWN ON HIS LUCK AND NEEDS WORK.

I WON'T LIE, I NEED A BEER.

Now in my fourth year at Windsor United Methodist Church, I was waiting for a couple the other night to show of up for pre-marriage counseling when I noticed a signer sitting in the median of University Avenue and 63rd street. The first thought that came to my mind was to see if I knew him, so I looked out the window. My next thought was how long it would take before somebody stopped to give him some money. I watched a good five minutes and not one car stopped to contribute to his begging. Then the next thought hit me, and I suspect it came from God. "BOB, WHAT'S KEEPING YOU FROM GOING OUT AND VISITING WITH HIM?" So I walked over to the wall in our church parking lot and called out to him, asking if he would come over to the parking lot. He got up and ran across the street, dodging cars. My first realization was that I had never seen him before. Then I read his sign, which was written on a piece of cardboard no larger than 15 inches by 15 inches. The sign read:

I AM HEADED TO ARKANSAS AND AM HUNGRY. CAN YOU SPARE 25 CENTS. I spoke with him a few moments and he assured me the money was not to purchase alcohol. I told him that it did not matter to me if that was what he needed; he could use the money as he decided. I handed him $4.00, which is not much for our family. I often spend that at a local restaurant having coffee in the morning. (Raises an ethical question, doesn't it? Which is the worse use of money: Giving $4.00 to a homeless man who may purchase some alcohol? Giving $4.00 for an over-priced cup of coffee?) I suspect on judgment day I know the answer to that one already, but then our lifestyles in this nation may also raise some questions as to how we have handled our resources when we stand before the Creator of the universe.

He then asked me where the nearest grocery store was located so he could buy some meat and bread. I sent him off to HyVee at 70th & University for his purchases. As I walked back to the church, the young couple was getting out of their car. They know me fairly well. They commented that they bet I gave him money.

I had noticed that not only did not one person stop to offer him any assistance, worse yet nobody even make eye contact for fear he might come up to their car. No one spoke to him. They acted as if he did not exist as they waited for the light to change so they could go on with their lives. A red light was an inconvenience as they had to slow down before heading into Windsor Heights. A red light was a chance for him to get a few coins. The red light was a chance for both parties to have made contact and visited for a few seconds. But then we are so uncomfortable with begging and such sights that we like to look away in the hope that the problem will disappear.

Poverty is not going to go away. You soon learn that people do what they have to do in order to survive. That is especially true if you are a female and have children. Parents will do what they never thought possible when their children have needs. I suggest to you that at a certain point in our existence, when need becomes critical, we do things we never thought we would ever do in our life.

Prostitution as a way of raising money.

Dining out of a dumpster on a hot summer day.

Holding a sign on the corner of 63rd & University.

I hope the next time you see homeless persons you will consider speaking an encouraging word to them as you pass them. I hope maybe you will at least risk making eye contact, letting them know you see them as a person. I really don't care if you give people money or not. That is an individual thing as God speaks to our heart with each situation. But looking away from problems in order to feel more comfortable is not the Christian response Jesus had in mind when he told us to feed the hungry, to clothe the naked, to visit those in prison.

The next time, see what conversation God has with you when you find yourself in a position where you are not quite sure how to respond.

*We and God have business with each other,
and in opening ourselves to His influence
our deepest destiny is fulfilled.*
-William James

My Worst Nightmare

Each of the staff at the Door of Faith Mission, along with other obligations that we might have, had one task we all shared. We were all expected to have a certain number of men on our case management list for whom we assumed responsibility. The number would vary from 15-20 men per staff person. As staff we were expected to meet with the men weekly for a half hour or so. In reality that was a goal but not always a task we could fulfill. The difficulties surrounding this part of the job related to which men were assigned to you. Some of the guys were simply delightful and the time flew by, while others would have rather endured a beating and so they would simply sit in the office until you told them the time was up. During my years, I on average would have one-two pedophiles on my case list. You could expect to spend one-two hours a week with these guys.

First of all, I had to monitor that they met their curfew at the Mission.

Second, one had to help them get a job and also make sure the job was appropriate for whatever convictions they may have had. This meant they could not be anywhere near children.

Third, I had to make sure they were in chapel service and counseling. They often wanted to attend a local church, which we prohibited. (After six months we might set up a program with a local church if the pastor was willing to take responsibility for the man. But we wanted time to see if they were for real in their faith or merely seeking a group of non-suspecting church members to which they might attach themselves).

Fourth, I would spend a great deal of time with the parole officer making sure that they were in compliance with all that was expected of them.

One parole officer (P.O.) was not a Christian and was up front about that from the start, and he also by his actions assured me that he did not have much respect for me either. Over the next six months, though, that would change as he began to give me more and more power in dealing with his client. He would later tell me that had it not been for me he would have thrown one of his clients in prison by revoking him months sooner. This man I will call Jack (which is not his name for reasons you can understand) would try my patience. He had worked his way into a rather fundamental church where the pastor believed that if he asked forgiveness and came to Jesus he was healed and safe to be in society. I suspect that pastor was one of the reasons his parole officer had such little trust in me.

I remember Jack coming back into my office one day and telling me he was cured. (We might cure a ham before eating, but I am not convinced that a pedophile is cured. At best they learn their triggers and they put a safety net into place where they hopefully can keep from offending). When he shared his new-found wisdom, we went around and around, at which point I phoned his P.O. and we all had a great come-to-Jesus meeting. Unfortunately, in a week or so, this guy was so manipulative and foolish that he came back in my office and shared that he had apologized to his victim and the victim's mother in front of the whole church. They then hugged at the pastor's encouragement and now things were fine.

It was like hitting your head against a block wall trying to get through to him that things were not fine and that it was not acceptable to break the court order that he have no contact with the person. He just could not get it that if the mom and child were in church he had to leave the building. We tried contracts. We tried agreements between all of us. He just would not listen or believe that he had to do the work in order to not go back to the prison system. Finally, one day I got a call from the P.O. telling me he had a meeting with Jack and that he was going to revoke him and send him back to prison and that I should not expect him back at the Door of Faith Mission. I was somewhat relieved, but also somewhat saddened. I had taken him out for his birthday to a buffet to celebrate his 20- something birthday. In some ways there were parts of this guy that I came to care for and see that God dearly loved.

Julie would tell me one day that God had spoken to her and that she needed to be kind to him and that he was one of God's children. Previously, Jack had been one of the guys she just could not stand to be around. Even when people have done terrible things and probably will do them again, they are still the same person that Jesus died for as He did for me and you. Jack would months later tell Rudy (a volunteer and friend of mine) that I was the reason Jack had shared with Rudy on a jail visit to another man that he was not going back to prison. Rudy told me, *"Bob, he just does not get it."*

When he left, another guy quickly found his way to my case load. I'll call him Tom. Tom only needed a job and all his problems would be fixed. We held to the same rules for him but he quickly found ways to work the system. He got a job that required him to be out later than his curfew and surely we would not want him to give up work. So we modified his curfew. He then met a friend and fell in love with her and wanted some time to be with her after curfew hours. We held tight to the curfew.

Then one Sunday morning he told me that he was spending more and more time with her and that even her children liked him. He had not mentioned that she had kids. I hit the roof and one of the few times I lost my control and screamed at any of the men happened that day. The deskman knocked on the office door to see what was happening and if I was okay. I also think he wanted to see if I was killing the man. Then Tom made the comment to me that he thought I had said that I wanted to help him. I still remember saying, *"I thought so, too!"* He was allowed to stay even though I had already kicked him out of the Mission. I took him back for one more try. A few weeks later I reached the point where we did not want to be a part of the fall-out that was coming and he was dismissed from the program.

Another guy came in one day and although he was still not sentenced, told me the details of what had happened and the charges that were coming. We went through the legal process and I was invited to attend court with him when his date came. The prosecutor knew me and was curious why I was there. His lawyer knew me from a previous church position and was shocked to see me there. But I had come to believe that Jesus would have been in court with them, not because he liked what they did. Jesus was willing to die for all, that we might know God's forgiveness. Certainly I could show that forgiveness by going to court with him that day. I recall the mom being on the stand and her testimony:

She had three children and the court asked if Bill (not his real name) was the father of the first or second or third child, and she assured the court Bill was not their dad.

The judge then asked her the name of the dad and she had no idea.

The judge asked her the name of the dad for the second child, and she only knew the first name.

The judge then asked her the name of the dad for the third child and she gave a name but had no idea where he lived.

Bill had been staying with her and also using drugs at the time of the sexual exploitation. One morning he came to and had been in bed with one of the children and he maintained it was only because he passed out there. (I tend to believe him). The court, though, had other intentions. They offered him a deal that he could walk on the charges if he accepted a no contact order and plead guilty to a misdemeanor. He wondered what I thought? My advice was to jump at the possibility of getting out of the mess with a slap on the hand.

Kids are so at risk when parents allow drugs and alcohol into the home. Usually when they are using drugs they also bring in a number of folks connected to the addictions who are not safe for anybody to be around. I can't think of one man who had come through our doors who had sex offenses in his criminal history that I would feel safe having around my children. With that said, I also do not believe the rules the legislature has placed into effect are keeping us safe. Many of the guys are living outside in the woods or at rest areas on the Interstate system or other places because they can't find a safe place to live that is not in violation of the current law.

There needs to be a place like the Mission, before it became illegal for them to have sex offenders on site, where somebody is managing the case. If people are to learn not to offend again they will need a lot more help and oversight than they are currently getting under the system. I also doubt that our prison system can handle the strain of the increased population as we seek to keep them behind bars for longer periods of time.

Of everything I did at the Mission, this area was probably the least appealing. But I also wonder if anything I did there was more productive than trying to keep society a bit safer while at the same time attempting to love the person who society had decided was beyond redemption. I am not soft on crime, but I also believe that regardless of what we have done, God still has the right to redeem the person. Even though God may redeem an individual, it does not mean the consequences of what he has done go away. If you are a parent, you better watch out for your child because the State of Iowa cannot protect the children from these individuals. You might want to clamp down on the computer in your home. If your children are on it unattended, regardless of their age, you have opened your home to the likes of Jack, Tom and Bill. Unfortunately, there are many more out there looking for their next victim.

I would have you learn this great fact: That a life of doing right is the wisest life there is.
-Proverbs 4:11

My Most Embarrassing Gift

One of my false assumptions was that I had something to offer the men at the Door of Faith Mission which would change their lives. (Some truth in that but not what I had envisioned in the beginning). Julie and I would come to understand over the years that the men had something to offer *us* that would completely change not only our lives but how we would see ourselves in ministry. I had assumed that it was about doing ministry for the men. God has always intended that we are to be in ministry together with one another. It is in shared ministry that we come to know God and the will of God in our lives. I would come to understand that God demanded and would accept nothing less than vulnerability on my part if I were to have any lasting effect upon those who came through my office door or whom I was to meet on the streets of Des Moines.

Initially in the job I saw myself as the giver and everyone else as the receiver. I am uncomfortable when people do things for me. I would much sooner be the one giving help than the one receiving assistance. It would be a difficult lesson to learn that the men had something to teach me.

I believe people have bought into the false assumption that we are in control of our lives and what happens in our lives. The truth is that when we act as if we are in control of our life, God is denied opportunities that might help us grow. Some things I did that were immature:

> *When I would take one of the men out for coffee, I always bought. (After all, they were homeless and had nothing to give me).
> *When men came to the office needing assistance, I

would give them money.

(After all, God tells us to give to the needy and these men appeared to be needy).

*One of the men was severely depressed. Julie and I invited him to our home for an overnight stay so he could get away from the Mission. He would grow to become a part of our family over the years.

(After all, we were called to be in ministry for those who are sick and need healing).

Looking back, much of what I did originated from great intentions. Unfortunately, in reality my actions had left me with a good feeling that I was doing God's work among the less fortunate of society. I now realize that much of what I did was not always in the best interest of those I had been called to serve. So often in the church we find ourselves doing things that stroke our own egos. We take the credit instead of giving credit to God.

I remember the first time I was out for coffee with one of the men and he wanted to pay for both of us. I saw that as his way of thanking me for our friendship. But I did not at the time see us as equals. I was the healer and he was the one in need of healing so it would not be acceptable for me to take a gift from him. He did not get to pay that day.

That night as I talked with Julie and told her of the happenings at the coffee shop, she completely surprised me by her response. She asked me why in the world I had not given him an element of pride and allowed him to pay when he asked to do so? As would be the case, many of the lessons I learned at the Mission came from my wife's instruction. The next time it happened, she thought I should accept the invitation. After all, people don't do what they don't want to do. She also asked me a question, *"How can you give to others if you won't let them return the giving back to you?"* I am still not completely comfortable with that in my life, but I did begin practicing gracious thanksgiving when someone offered me a gift.

We had been at the Mission some four to five years when the incident happened that completely changed my preconceived notion of who was in charge. I came to understand that night how God uses people, all people, even the homeless to change the hard-hearted lives of people, all people, even Chaplains. We had been having a difficult time over some issues surrounding family. Work had also started to become more of a job than a calling and it must have become apparent to some of the men. They have a great sense of reading people and who they are. You don't survive on the street unless you can tell who is your friend and who is real as opposed to those who only play games.

Often they would come and tell me things that later turned out to be true. They could see through folks way before I in my limited sense of intelligence had deduced the truth in others. My greatest struggle at the time was also with some staff situations and internal things at the Mission. Whenever I struggled, it was never related to the men. My struggles over the years would be with decisions of the administration and what they felt the ministry should look like. EXAMPLE: We would be informed that illegal aliens could not stay at the Mission nor could we provide ministry to them. Brother Patrick (Patrick was a Catholic Monk who worked part time at the Mission and happened to share an office with me), and I expressed gratitude that Jesus did not work at the mission because he would not have tolerated such a foolish command. For a time the administration backed down on that rule. Whatever was going on, several of the men picked up on it and decided to do something about it.

It was March 11, which happens to be my birthday, and it fell on a Tuesday. Julie and I were at the Mission eating supper before we shared in the evening devotional time in the chapel. They had gotten the cook to bake a birthday cake to celebrate my birthday that evening. They brought the cake out and the men sang happy birthday to me. Then they presented a birthday card to me that night. I opened the card and found myself speechless. Inside the card was $40.00 in cash with the instructions to take Julie out to dinner and get away. They also included in the card two nights stay at the Cottage Bed & Breakfast here in Des Moines. The card stated: *We know you are tired and need to get away and we want you to take time for you and Julie, Happy Birthday.*

Here are some 78 men living at the Mission because they don't have enough money to rent an apartment or buy the things they need for themselves. And yet they had made the effort of collecting money to purchase us this gift. I am still a little embarrassed by the generosity of those men that night. It was not the gift that so changed my life. It was the love they had for us that showed me what God expects of us in all our dealings with people each and every day.

We need to be open to people and their needs.

We are called to ministry to those who are hurting.

We are expected to love folks regardless of their status in life.

In turn God promises that lives will be changed. I said at the beginning I had expected to change lives when I started working at the Mission. I believe that did happen but not in the way I had expected. I also had expected others to be changed because of me. What was a shock was the way they would transform *my* life and how I see other people. That did not happen overnight, nor is the transformation complete. My life is one of continual struggle, seeking to know and understand God more fully. One thing I have learned, though, is we must get outside the walls of the church to be in ministry that changes the lives of people. At Windsor United Methodist Church we seek to be in ministry so that others can change our lives.

I recall a person telling me how our mission group hoped to touch people on the first trip we took together after Julie and I arrived at Windsor. I recall the strange look on that person's face when I said we would not change anybody that much the week we went to Pine Ridge Indian Reservation. But I assured the mission group that God would change them. They had the same look of disbelief that I had when I started to work at the Mission. On the way home, though, they had a different look as God had begun a new work in them through association with those who lived on the Reservation.

Are you open to what God can do in *your* life if you give up control? It won't be comfortable but I assure you it will be life changing. If you are ready to feel God's presence, go and commit to some mission work and you will be blessed.

Your daily life is your temple and your religion.   *-Kahlil Gibran*

Black Outs

Todd arrived at the old Door of Faith Mission, located at 1006 Grand Avenue in Des Moines, around lunchtime and wondered if he could check in. He had heard out east that this was a real working man's Mission where you could get work and also have a place to stay. We checked Todd in and he put his name on the work list. (The work list was a paper the men signed at 5:00 p.m. each day for the jobs that would come into the Mission the next day. They were required to work while maintaining a pleasant attitude so as to present the Mission in good light. In turn, the employers were asked to treat the men with respect and to avoid profanity around them as well as not offering them drugs or alcohol. At the end of the day they would pay the men cash as agreed upon and bring the men back to the Mission).

The job Todd got was at Michael's Restaurant and he needed to catch the bus to the site. He is directionally challenged and was having a hard time understanding how to get there. It was almost the end of the day and I was headed up to catch the bus so I offered to walk him to the bus and help him get on the right one. Todd and I would be friends from that day on. He would tell people, *"I just could not believe one of the staff would take the time to help me find my way when they did not even know me."*

We did camp-outs at our home outside of Adel, Iowa (located near Des Moines) and up to 12 men would spend the weekends from time to time. On one such night we had eaten and Julie and I went to bed while the men talked around the fire ring near the tents. We left the back door open so they could come in and use the restrooms, with the instructions that the next morning whoever got up first was to start the coffee pot. Sometime around 2:00

79

a.m., we heard talking in the kitchen. Todd and another man had made coffee and decided to finish off the leftover pie before the other guys woke up and came in for breakfast. It was funny hearing them in the kitchen, acting like a bunch of youth as they talked and joked. We came to understand that at the time the men started to drink, their development stalled. So when they would stop drinking and found sobriety, often they acted a great deal like the age they were when they first started to abuse the substances. This would be one of many times that Todd would be in our home and included as a part of our family.

He had drunk for years (25 plus). Todd would have periods of sobriety but they never seemed to last. He was able to make it six months at a time and then he would just go off the deep end and drink until everything he had saved up was lost. One time I remember going to his apartment to encourage him to go to the hospital for detox. He was still not finished with the bout of alcohol and refused, threatening to beat me up if I did not leave. Todd was not a fighter.

One time I found him lying on the sidewalk, drunk, and he wanted me to pick him up so he could hit me. I knew that even drunk he would never lay a hand on me. I knelt in front of him and told him I wanted him to come with me to the hospital and he started to hit me on the legs. (Hit is a strong word in that my three-year-old grandchild packs more of a punch than he did). Later, when he sobered up and another guy told him what he had done, he was humiliated by his actions. When he stopped drinking, Todd was like most of the men and shame would just flood over them with sadness for their actions. Unfortunately for the families that had to see them during the times they were drunk, the words spoken and the actions inflicted did not go away as easily. Most families would find they could only endure so much and they would then pull back and limit contact with the substance abuser.

To show the severity of addiction, I share the following story. I had received a tape from a mission out east. The tape showed some of their ministry and at the end issued an appeal to help them continue the work they were doing. Most financial tapes were similar in their appeals. The unique item as I watched it was that Todd was in the picture. He was leaning against the building waiting to go in and eat dinner at their site. Later in the week I asked him when he had been to that city? Todd told me, "*I have never been to that state let alone that city.*" I invited him to come with me to the canteen. I put the tape in after telling him he had a double that looked just like him. We played the tape. Todd then responded, "*I'll be _____, that's me, but I don't remember ever being there.*" He would start drinking in one city and end up across the country when he came out of the black outs.

One such time when he was really drinking I encouraged him sober up and to come to our home after Julie and I had moved back into Des Moines. I did not realize at the time he was in a black out. I knew he was really drunk and I hoped to avoid the mess that comes with it, so I offered to have him sleep if off in our back porch. I set him up in a recliner and I laid out my sleeping bag on the porch floor in case he needed something. I asked him to give me all his money since he was threatening to go drink again. He would later apologize, saying, "*Bob, I always keep a $20.00 bill in my sock for such times as this.*" The next morning, after accepting his apology, I offered him mine. "*Todd, remember last night when you wanted directions downtown so you could walk back when I would not take you? Well, I actually gave you the directions to Saylorville Lake instead. I decided that if you wanted to drink I was going to send you out in the country where I knew you could not find anything to drink.*"

81

I had hoped that our love helped him overcome his addictions. It didn't, unfortunately. There would be times of sobriety. We met his family after a year of not drinking when they stopped by our home to meet us. I also attended his wedding when he remarried, hoping for a new start. He eventually left Des Moines and settled back in his home state near his son and ex-wife, where he started to attend church. He would work in their food pantry, volunteering after he retired. Todd attended church and church school in an attempt to understand the love of Jesus he was sure he did not deserve.

That may have been his greatest struggle; trying to figure out how God could still love him after all he had done to those who loved him. He was just not able to let go of the guilt that held him so close in bondage. It has been more than a year since we have heard from him and that is not good news. I also know, as with many of the men, the chance is strong we may never hear from him again. He may die in some city alone and be buried without anyone ever knowing he died. Todd always told me that he needed a change of scenery in the hope of staying sober. But when he arrived in the new community and woke up, he found he had brought himself along as well. He would say, "*I just am not able to get away from myself and I always bring my problems with me.*"

It is a real mystery why God would have created the earth, knowing full well the day of creation how his creatures would live out their lives.

It is a real mystery how God can still love us after all the terrible things we have done to one another.

It is a mystery beyond comprehension that God would have chosen the likes of us to carry the message to a hurting world. God, I am not sure I would have entrusted such a gift to the likes of me, and yet that is what you based your hopes of the world upon. Jesus came to show us love, knowing that some of the creation would take on that love and share it with others. Over the years my greatest joy at the Mission was that of being able to love and care for some of God's creation who did not yet know or believe that love was available to them. I have no doubt that Todd came to know and experience the love of God. But he was just not able to find the healing he was so desperately seeking. Healing that would take away the guilt that was so deep in his soul. My prayer is that others in other cities will be there when God brings Todd into their presence, and the seed we have been allowed to sow will take root and grow.

Each of the men who came through those doors touched our lives in ways I would never have thought possible. Some touched us by the gift of their love. Others would touch me by showing the hardness of my heart and my desperate need for God that I might love them. You may have seen me with tears in my eyes when people like Todd would come back to the Mission drunk and I realized that the cycle of suffering for him was still not complete.

I know that each of you have people in your lives who are just as desperate for healing and that God will use you as well to bring the peace of Jesus to them. God bless you.

A certain man went down from Jerusalem to Jericho, and fell among thieves, which stripped him of his raiment and wounded him, and departed leaving him half dead.

And by chance there came down a certain priest that way; and when he saw him, he passed by on the other side. And likewise, a Levite, when he was at the place, came and looked on him, and passed by on the other side.

But a certain Samaritan, as he journeyed, came where he was: and when he saw him, he had compassion on him. And went to him, and bound up his wounds, pouring in oil and wine, and set him on his own beast, and brought him to an inn, and took care of him.

Take care of him; and whatsoever thou spendest more, when I come again, I will repay thee.

Which of these three, thinkest thou, was the neighbor unto him that fell among the thieves?   *-Jesus of Nazareth*

How Did It Get Like This?

It is amazing how families become so estranged that they cease to even communicate with one another. How sad to witness as a pastor in your congregation those families that have fought to the point where they refuse to be in the same room with other members of their biological family. At some points I have even heard of them breaking out into fist fights at the funeral services of parents. Until my time at the Mission, my feelings were mostly of sadness that things had gotten to such a point and I felt tremendous sympathy for the combatants. It occurred to me often that the chances for world peace are really limited when we can't even tolerate our own siblings and neighbors. It seems to me that those of us in the Christian Church have not taken the words of Jesus very seriously when he said:

> *"Love your neighbor as yourself."*
> *"Pray for those who persecute you."*
> *"Forgive your enemies."*

But when I went to the Mission, I began to see first hand how this hard-hearted spirit affected people, and my heart broke. I pray this may break your heart as well if you find yourself separated from family.

Robert always sat alone when he ate dinner in the dining area, unless it was when others stopped by just to annoy him with their teasing. It usually did not take much to really get him upset. He went to work right after breakfast and returned in time for the evening meal. He also had a part-time job which took him out evenings for several hours during the summer months. He worked for an individual for very little money but it was a place where he could remain sober. Some five years before, the medical staff had convinced him that if he did not stop drinking he

87

would soon be dead. Unlike many of the oldtime drinkers, he took the medical advice seriously and never touched alcohol again. But that doesn't mean his life changed a great deal.

When you looked at Robert, he appeared to be really unhappy. He seldom smiled or spoke to people, with few exceptions. Those exceptions for the most part did not include me. I would from time-to-time stop by and eat with him, trying to break through the hard exterior, but I had little success. I did learn that his favorite meal was liver and onions. Until I met him, that would not have been a choice that I would have picked, but over the years I actually came to tolerate it. My wife always came on Tuesday evenings for dinner and would stay for chapel services at the Mission, this giving her time to know the men.

I am not sure how, but Robert told her a bit about himself and that his favorite pie was rhubarb pie. (As grumpy as he appeared that should have made sense). One of my tasks at the Mission was to remember the men's birthdays by giving them a card and also a gift. We had lots of donations and the gifts usually included a new shirt or some item of clothing. Often the response was that they had not had a birthday gift in years and tears would even accompany their accepting of the small token.

It was important, we found, to remember the times in the men's lives when family would have been there to let them know they were special. Robert was never moved much outwardly by the card or gift, at least until Julie decided to make him a rhubarb pie for his birthday. She gave it to him one night at dinner. The guys who often teased him went over and asked if he was not going to share with them some of his good fortune. NO! (A real simple answer).

But we noticed that a change began to appear in his

life after that small token. He started to visit with Julie when she would come on Tuesday and Sundays for dinner and then the worship services. He never did find himself attending worship or Bible study, though; after all, pie only goes so far. Robert did, though, start to open up with me as well. I suppose he thought that if Julie was that nice she must have seen something in me he had not noticed yet. We would begin talking in the canteen, where they could hang out and smoke and watch t.v. Over dinner we would visit about things we like and did not like, as well as where we grew up.

He was older, which is unusual in that the men are often dead by 60 years of age due to their life-style, but he had made it longer.

He told me his family came from the Dakota area. One day he also told me they had a family cemetery plot there and that he would like to be buried there with them. In our conversations I asked if he would mind being taken there in the back of my pickup truck with the topper? That seemed acceptable and I told him I would be willing to drive his body up there if we could make arrangements with the funeral home when he died. For some reason we began to talk about family and he told us that he had one brother but had lost touch with him years ago (20 years). He thought maybe he lived in the Minneapolis area but was not sure after so many years. The Mission secretary and others did some research on the web and came up with a name and phone number. Sure enough, that was his brother and they talked for awhile and Robert told him where he was.

Several weeks later the lost brother made a trip to Des Moines and they spent several days together visiting and discussing their past. It seems this brother had gotten married a long time ago and Robert did not especially care for the new wife. I can only imagine how he must have made the displeasure known to his sibling. (It is funny, when we get married that we don't take kindly to comments about our spouse). They had broken off all communications and Robert had left the area. However, they had a good time together when his brother visited Des Moines and his brother told him he would be back in a month when he passed through the area on business.

Unfortunately, when I called him several days later it was to let him know his brother had died. He told me that had he known how ill his brother was he would have stayed. Julie and I visited after all of this and marveled how God works through events and brings healing in our lives when we open to that experience. A small rhubarb pie had opened the door to a man who had built so many walls to protect himself from the world, so he would not be hurt anymore. Those walls, though, rather than protecting had really isolated him where he spent many years alone at the Mission in Des Moines with few friends. He was not grumpy. He was not mean. He just kept up a facade to protect himself from the stupidity of others at the Mission while he tried to live out his life.

What a miracle in our lives to be a small part in this connection between siblings. That thing Jesus said about "*Forgiving*" I am firmly convinced He meant with no exceptions. God's heart breaks when we live in the sin of anger and separation from one another and ultimately from God.

The older brother made arrangements for Robert's body to be shipped back home to be buried with the other members of their family. Robert's travels took him a long way from home but he did eventually make it back to the family that loved and nurtured him as a little boy.

People would often ask me how I did the job at the Mission without getting burned-out, when so many of the men would return to drinking. It is because I got to see miracles God performed there through men such as Robert. I got to be a part of the people's lives as they restored broken relationships with family and with God. I was blessed to see some men turn their lives around and find meaning, which they had all but given up on ever happening in this existence. You don't get burned out doing things you love. You burn-out when your life has no meaning and you live in isolation from this hurting world in the false hope of protecting yourself. I learned through those years to become vulnerable and in the vulnerability I learned about strength.

I want to ask you several questions and then I have a request:

Do you have anyone you are estranged from right now?

Is there someone you are holding a grudge against?

Is there some sin you need to ask forgiveness for from another person?

WILL YOU CALL THEM TODAY AND SEEK THE MIRACLE OF

GOD'S RESTORATION IN YOUR OWN LIFE AS WELL?

I have made calls like the one I am requesting of you. Sometimes it worked out well. There are other times when all I got was peace in knowing I did what is expected from God. But there is a peace the world can't give that is waiting for you if you will only live in harmony with Jesus.

All the beautiful sentiments in the world weigh less than a single lovely action.
-John Ruskin

Don't Bet on It

Who would have believed that gambling would become so pervasive in the State of Iowa as what we are now experiencing? When I was a youth in northeast Iowa, they hauled off the local priest for having a gaming weekend at the church and put him on trial. One used to think that you had to go to Las Vegas in order to find the joy of giving your money away to organized crime. Now, if you suggest we call it gambling, you are considered politically incorrect, according to the State of Iowa, which much prefers the title of Gaming. *"Go ahead and have some fun anyway."*

I have to admit that gambling has never been much of an issue for me personally. When I was a pastor in Dallas Center for nine years, I even joined many of the men from the local church in pools at the local bowling alley while we had coffee waiting for the Post Office to open, so I could pick up the mail and head to the office. On a good day you lost. If you happened to win, it cost you more for coffee and donuts than you received, so I hardly call that gambling. I knew that if I won I still lost. There is some truth to that wisdom even today.

One morning the men were buying the scratch lottery tickets and for some reason I happened to buy one. The unfortunate thing (or fortunate turn of events, depending how you consider the results) is that I won $50.00. I took the money, bought a round of coffee for the 20- some guys there that morning, and forgot the whole thing. That is until I got a call from my District Superintendent. He had read in the local paper about my winnings and he was upset that I would be gambling.

It was not much of a concern to me so I said he could be upset but it was none of his business, but thanks for the call anyway. It would happen a few weeks later that the issue would become personal for me. I was visiting Grace Rhodes, who happened to be a member of the church, and a person I really valued for her spiritual leadership and commitment to Christ. We had grown extremely close over the years as I helped her through problems surrounding her husband's illness and death. She, too, had read the notice in the paper. In about as loving a way as she could muster, she informed me that she was embarrassed by her pastor for taking part in such an activity. I have never bought a lottery ticket since that time, not because it is a concern for me but because of how others might be affected by my actions.

It would be years later that I would be confronted, while living in the Adel area while serving as chaplain at the Mission. An old parishioner attending the Sweet Corn Days Festival in Adel sought my support for a new casino that would open near the strip clubs off Highway 90. I refused to sign their petition and stated why I would not. His negative personal comments toward me at that time became the initiative for some of us to create a group to fight the casino from entering Dallas County. I co-chaired the "Don't Float the Boat" committee that, along with God's help, prevented Dallas County from entering the gambling business with its own casino.

You see, it was while working at the Mission I was beginning to observe the first-hand cost of gambling in the lives of those men living there. We were beginning to connect gambling with other addictions. They might stop using alcohol and drugs while at the Mission, but we noticed that they purchased extreme amounts of scratch tickets. The Mission staff would eventually make it illegal to possess scratch tickets on site. This was in response to the men buying $10-20 worth of them at a time and bringing them back to the Mission to see if they had a winner. We felt–out of respect for many of our contributors–it was inappropriate to have the men gambling in a facility which was paid for by many dollars coming from church funds.

Examples of what I saw over those years:

1. At times I would go to the local restaurant for coffee with men so we could talk in privacy outside the confines of the Mission. I would watch the folks living on the streets, who could not afford an apartment, scratching 40-50 tickets in the hope of hitting it big. They would tell me at the time, "*I can't win if I don't play.*" Do those words sound familiar? (That was one of the leading advertising slogans of the Iowa Lottery at the time.)

2. I was stopping in Albion one day at the local Casey Store on the way to my folks. I was delayed as a woman turned in her $20.00 in winnings and waited to be paid. She asked for the winnings in more tickets. She then told the clerk that she had spent her whole disability check on tickets in the hope of hitting it big. When she left, I asked the clerk if I could have the pile of non-winning tickets she left behind. They gave them to me and I used them as a poster when speaking against gambling at churches.

3. I was asked to speak one day at another United Methodist Church during the Sunday worship service. I had planned to tell about the high cost of addictions. I had material pertaining to alcohol/drugs/gambling. But before I got up to speak, they had a special appeal for the congregation to buy the $1 chances on a quilt they were raffling off to raise money for the local United Methodist Women. I sat there for a moment wondering if I should change my sermon, and

decided against it. I shared some material and then gave the editorial comment that gambling was prohibited by the United Methodist Church, of which I am an elder. As I talked, one woman rose to her feet and began applauding. I can only imagine that the aforementioned Grace Rhodes might have been happy watching how her words had changed a young pastor who now has guts to speak the truth.

4. One man told me that he had inherited $60,000 from his family when they died. He and his wife took the money to Las Vegas and lost the whole amount in three days. He then went on to say it was the best three days of his life. (Something is wrong with that).

5. I have a close friend who is a compulsive gambler and it has taken him all across the country in pursuit of riches, only to return broke and discouraged after each experience.

6. We had a young man who worked for Principal Financial Services living at the Mission. Each pay period he would take the bus to the Indian casino near Tama and Stay until he was broke. He would return to the mission and work his grant job for room and board while also working at Principal. He would slip in the back door after work so no one at Principal would see him and question him while he lived there.

7. We had a young college student living with us who had lost everything due to gambling. He especially loved to hustle pool games. He had his own customized pool stick and made a lot of money at it. But he lost even more money on other forms of gambling. He just could not stop even though he spent much time in treatment.

I came to realize that gambling is one of those addictions that is hard to control. It destroys families, individuals and even affects communities when people begin stealing the money to support the habit. You may think gambling is acceptable. You may even like to go out to Prairie Meadows for an evening of relaxation and enjoyment. (And you might not have a problem with that or spend more than you can afford). But there are many in this nation who cannot control themselves and we as taxpayers end up paying for their addictions. What we don't pay for is the emotional cost of families destroyed in the process; we just don't experience what it does to the lives of those involved.

I have been in Prairie Meadows a few times. You see, I am not above going to the place when I know a guy is there and seeking him out and asking him if he won't leave and come back with me. The last time I did while working at the Mission, I was walking through the building and I heard my name called out. I turned and there was another man from the Mission who just wanted to say hello to me and was curious as to why I was there. I told him I was looking for a person, and we visited a few moments. I didn't stay long because one thing I can't stand is cigarette smoke in a confined area and what it does to my eyes. I did find the person in the parking lot and he looked exactly like others who have been on a three-day binge with alcohol. He had been up for more than 48 hours straight, seeking to hit his fortune and was broke and really depressed with no idea of what to do. It is at that point I put my arms around him and say that God loves him and so do I. *"LET'S GO HOME"*.

I am not usually politically active as a pastor. I believe there is little room in the church for political action, but I am convinced that gambling is an exception. In few other decisions the State of Iowa has made do we promote active addiction of our citizens so the wealthy in our area can avoid paying more for taxes to support the things we feel we can't do without. Gambling is clearly a direct tax on the poor. I recall one conversation with a man who was scratching lottery tickets one day while we were drinking coffee. I had asked him why he wasted his money on them?

He responded by asking me some questions:

"Bob, do you have a home?"
"Do you have a car?"
"Do you have a family?"

He knew the answers would be yes.

He then told me that unless he hit it big he would never be able to afford such things. He has bought into the state-sponsored lie that gambling is the only way the poor can ever make it in this world. That is why they spend money putting billboards and advertising in areas that promote gambling where only the poor live. WHEN is the last time you saw a billboard in or around the area of Glen Oaks (a new and wealthy housing division outside of Des Moines) asking people to gamble? It won't happen because the rich know that you don't make money at Prairie Meadows.

Dreams don't come true in Altoona, Iowa, at the race track.

It is not enough merely to exist...for remember, you don't live in a world all your own. Your brothers are here, too. The only things that count in life are the imprints of love which we leave behind us after we are gone.

-Albert Schweitzer

Pen Pals

I have known Tim for a good 12 years now, a relationship that started while I was working at the Door of Faith Mission. Tim was one of those persons who was really easy to like and even easier to hate, depending on the day. His addictions had completely gained control of his life so that even when he wanted to do the right thing, he did the wrong. It so often seemed that the very thing he didn't want to do he did, and the very thing he knew he should do was the exact opposite of what transpired.

It would be a real stretch of the imagination to say that he had friends among his peers. His life was such that he was not able to be a friend to others, and yet there was a decent streak inside of him that would shine forth from time to time. I remember one day a person telling me they had seen him throw a rock and hit someone riding a bike down the street, just for pure meanness. (I recall thinking to myself that I would be careful to not ever turn my back on him).

He was in and out of the Mission so many times we lost track of the number of stays he had there. He was one of those individuals who elicited much discussion among the staff each time he returned. Carl, who was the director of the Mission for a number of years that I worked there, had a soft spot in his heart for Tim and just didn't seem to be able to say no to him. So Tim would return and in a week he would be asked to leave due to unacceptable behavior.

But it was during those stays that we started to become better acquainted. Part of the things we shared was no doubt Tim's belief that I was an easy mark and that he could put it over on me, and yet even with suspicion I started to care for him as I learned his story. That would be a lesson for me over the years, that as I came to know the men the outward actions played less of a part in how I saw them. It reminds me that God looks on the inside and sees what we can become while the world looks at the outside and sees what we appear to be. I guess I saw some of the hope in Tim that I believe God also saw in him.

Tim called me one day to ask a favor. His request was also cloaked in my promising him I would not call the police, letting them know he was coming to see me. He was high at the time and with his drug of choice, paranoia was out of control. He had been sentenced to drug treatment as a condition of release. He had planned to go to Denver and spend a year at their farm site where they had an extended long-term drug program through the Denver Rescue Mission. But as life was with Tim, he just never seemed to get around to doing the right thing. He was at the end of his rope, or close, when he called and asked to meet with me. His request was for me to drive him up north to his sponsor from AA. The sponsor had agreed to take him to Nevada, a small Iowa city, so he could turn himself in to the Story County authorities and hopefully be sent off to treatment instead of prison. I remember meeting Tim and visiting for a while before we drove north. Later on, I never gave it any more thought, assuming he was in the county jail and would be given some time to clean up.

Julie and I were getting ready to go on vacation and about to leave town when I heard on the evening news that Tim _____ was being sought in conjunction with a murder on the north side of Des Moines. I remember telling Julie that just could not be right; he was in jail and I re-told her the story. I looked up the sponsor's phone number and called him, asking if he had not taken Tim to the county jail. He, too, had heard the report and was saddened. He had indeed taken him to Nevada and they had talked for

104

some time outside the jail. He was getting ready to walk Tim into the jail but Tim assured him that he did not need for him to do so, that he would go check himself into the jail. The sponsor watched Tim walk in and so he had driven off, assuming Tim would follow through. Unfortunately, Tim had decided between the door and the officer's desk that he was not able to leave the drugs alone for the upcoming time he would be behind bars, and he left the facility.

In an attempt to elude capture, he had secured a car and together with another person, headed south toward the Mexican border in the hope of crossing into Mexico to escape the consequences of his actions. He was filling up the car somewhere in Texas when the local police spotted the car he was driving and they came up and made the arrest. With guns drawn he was thrown to the pavement in much the way we see on the TV show: "Cops". Tim found himself arrested for murder and in jail waiting his return to the Polk County jail.

Something strange began to happen in his life. Tim had made multiple professions of faith over the years, accepting Jesus Christ as his Savior. Previously, he had never permitted his sinful lifestyle to die, but now he was seeking the path to his own cross. He started to visit with the chaplain in the jail and somehow Jesus spoke to him through this person. I remember on one of my visits with him at the jail he informed me of what he planned to do. He believed that it was in his best interest to plead guilty to the charges and ask the court to forgo his pre-sentence hearing and to ask the judge to sentence him to life in prison. I encouraged him to consider what he was doing before making such an extreme decision that would affect him until death.

Tim was convinced that he needed to make amends for his actions. He also had some reluctance about going to court and having everything come out about the crime, both for his sake when he went to prison but more so for the sake of the family of the deceased. He told me that he just could not stand to have the crime scene pictures shown to the family in court and for them to hear everything that had happened. (A year later he would mail me a seven-page description of all that happened that day, giving me a blow-by-blow account of how he had murdered this man. He told me in his letter that if we were to continue our friendship over the years, he had to know that I could forgive him. I did read the material, but nothing included in that made God's offer of forgiveness void that I could see, nor did it give me a reason to judge Tim).

I suspect he was relieved to hear my answer when I responded to his letter. He also told me he would like me to use the testimony any time I wanted if it would help another person avoid the mistakes he had made. I remember a few days later hearing on WHO radio the report of Tim's confession and request that they immediately sentence him to prison for life. That is not how the court system usually works, but the judge agreed and he was sent off to the state prison system. I also remember WHO telling Tim's reason for requesting such a decision from the court. He had stated in court that he had done such terrible things in his life that he was scared to stand in front of God on judgment day with any more reasons for God to be angry at him. This was his first act of repentance for the way he had lived his life. That one act was convincing to me that his acceptance of Christ while in the Polk County jail was authentic.

Tim's confession of sin was finally followed by actions that did not benefit him but was for the benefit of others. He was beginning to learn that accepting Christ is not a way out of trouble but merely a path toward a new way of living and dealing with people. I recall even now sadness as I talked to Julie:

"I should have taken him to the Story County jail myself and walked him in."

"Why is it people have to have their lives and others destroyed before they change and begin to let Jesus have control?"

"What could I have done that might have saved his life and the life of this other man?"

It occurs to me now that Tim was never going to live his life on the outside as God intended for him to do. He had started smoking and drinking before the age of 10. He had moved on to grass and then meth as he aged. In order to pay for this habit, he had started down a path of destruction that hurt everyone who got in his way. Tim has started doing Bible study for real behind bars. He has started reading through the Bible, seeking its direction for his life. When confronted by violence in prison, he has started to turn the other cheek, even when he was not completely in the wrong. He did time in the hole rather than tell who had beaten him. (That is probably a good idea practically as well as living out his Christian life). Tim has several people who write to him in prison regularly now, but he has asked me if I know of others who might want to take up letter writing. Several guys I write to tell me that the letters in prison really help pass the time and keep up their spirits.

The Methodists under John Wesley's leadership had to visit people in jail or be kicked out of the fellowship. I would love to pass on to Tim names of any who like to make a commitment to write for life to a man behind bars. Give me a call if this might be one of your ministries to which God is calling you. I still have sadness as I think back on Tim or look at his picture when he was seven years old and sitting on a picnic table. I wonder what might have been had someone been able to intervene when he was

107

young? That is a motivation for me today to find the Tims of the world as God calls me to give my life to those who need love the most.

There is a destiny that makes us brothers,
None goes his way alone;
All that we send into the lives of others
Comes back into our own.

I care not what his temples or his creeds,
One thing holds firm and fast-
That into his fateful heap of days and deeds
The soul of man is cast.
                    -Edwin Markham

Who Ya Gonna Call?
Not the Police!

Over the years I was amazed at the restraint the Des Moines police would show when they dealt with calls concerning the men who either lived at the Door of Faith Mission or those homeless men who would come our way from time to time. I have seen the police yelled at, called names, threatened but seldom did I ever see them respond to insults in any way but professionally, and with great restraint. I would like to share a few memorable experiences that I had with regard to law enforcement.

The Capital Police Called:

One afternoon I had a call put through to me from the Capital Police asking if I would be interested in picking up one of the men who had listed the Mission as his address. If I would be willing to come get him, they would just as soon not take him downtown to book him and fill up the city jail. They said Henry had been found drunk on the second floor of the old historical building, passed out. The problem was they found him in the second floor women's restroom on a couch. They were charging him with public intoxication and he had agreed to show up for the court appearance, but they saw no reason to lock him up overnight. I agreed to come get him.

After picking him up, it became my problem to find a place for him to sleep off the effects of his drinking episode. I told him it would be at least the next day before he was sober and could return to the Mission, so we had to find a place for him to spend the night. He had no money and I had no intentions of taking him home with me. We settled upon Water Works Park. I drove him way out back in the woods where no one was likely to find him or where he would be likely to bother anybody else that afternoon and night. He had close to $1,000 worth of C.D.s, a Walkman Player and gold jewelry that he liked to wear. I suggested that if he trusted me it might be a good idea for me take that back to the Door and lock it up in the safe so he did not lose it or get mugged while he was drunk. He agreed. So I tucked him in for the night and went back to secure his property.

Secret Service:

Every now and then the President of the United States decides to come to Des Moines and that really ties up traffic when he proceeds to his downtown hotel from the airport. When the Mission was located at 10th & Grand, we were by the route that the President and his procession had to use most days. Things would change. I came in the Door of Faith Mission one day to find the Secret Service all over the building. They had found one of our guys who had made some unfortunate comments downtown. He apparently was not a supporter of the President and had commented that somebody should just walk up and hit him over the head. That is not a comment that the Secret Service considered acceptable. Anyway, they were talking of locking him up to keep the President safe. I remember commenting, *"He is not going to hurt anybody; he is just nuts."*

The day ended with their making him stay inside the building until the President left town. They also assured him they would be back and lock him up for a long time if he was not able to stay inside and keep his mouth shut.

Des Moines Police Department:

Have you ever wondered where the police are when you need them?

Have you ever wondered why there are so many when they are the last you want to see?

One of the guys asked me a favor. He had an old car

out back in the parking lot of the Mission. We did not allow the guys to park there during the day when the staff used the spots, so they had to find a meter or someplace else to leave their cars. It appeared that his car was hard to start and he had no place to leave it. He was wondering, since I was in charge at the time of the halfway houses on Buchanan Street, if I would let him store it there for a couple of weeks till he got some money to fix it up. I was not always the sharpest knife in the drawer and sometimes I promised things before thinking through the consequences. I agreed it would be acceptable for a couple of weeks. He then wondered if I would follow him to the storage location so I could give him a ride back to the Mission?

We set off to re-locate his car. We headed east down Locust street past the new Historical Building and turned left, going by the Capitol complex. The traffic was heavy. Just as we started up the hill, he pulled over and parked the car on the side of the road. I stopped behind him, turned on my blinkers and walked up to see what was wrong. Here's what he told me:

He was out of gas.

He had no driver's license.

The car was not his.

It was registered to another person.

He had no insurance.

He added that the police were pulling up right behind my car at that moment.

Mercy! I was helping to transport a stolen car! The driver had no license, no insurance, no registration, and the policeman was not happy, which I could tell by the look on his face as he approached us. I told the man to keep his mouth shut and let me do the talking.

I explained to the policeman who I was and that I was helping move the car for one of the men from the Mission to our half way-house. We visited and the officer never once asked the man for his license, registration, insurance or any other information. Moreover, he even offered to push the car out of the way.

Off we went as the policeman started to push the car for a block to get it out of the way. The man from the Mission, on the other hand, decided to just keep going and let the officer push his car another six blocks to the halfway houses. When we got there, he preceded to let him push the car down the alley. I could tell the policeman was not happy so I parked in front of the homes and jumped out of the car and ran around back through the yard to meet them. I was quick to thank him for all his help and assured him I could handle it from here. Off he went, hoping to never see us again.

As a staff person at the Mission, I came to really respect and appreciate the police force that protects us. On so many occasions they went out of their way, assisting us in getting men to the hospital. They often came when men were out of control and helped subdue them and sometimes even helped remove them from the building when they refused to go. I know the Mission was not a highlight in their day when they received the call, but they did a great job. Sometimes we don't express our appreciation enough with those who help us. Take a minute today to express thanks to someone who has gone out of his or her way to assist you

Make it a rule, and pray God to help you to keep it, never, if possible, to lie down at night without being able to say, "I have made one human being at least a little wiser, a little happier or a little better this day."
                    -Charles Kingsley

The High Price of Forgiveness

The years come and go and as Pastor I hear the same questions so many times that I have found myself inadvertently giving the same answers over and over. Many times we spew out the acceptable theological terminology without every considering what the person might really have going on in his or her life that caused the question in the first place. I have come to wonder if it is not better to leave the initial question unanswered while asking other questions of my own. Jesus had such a way of listening to people and drawing out of them their deepest need. The next time you are too busy to give a person the time they are asking, I invite you to consider the following story:

Although not my main task at the Mission, I did from time to time do intakes of new residents. That included meeting with them for a half hour or so, depending on what they were sharing at the time, and making the judgment whether they fit the program of the Mission. It was one such Sunday afternoon when the Intake Desk Man informed me there was a man who wanted to enter the Mission and needed to have an interview. Sunday afternoons were usually slower than other days so maybe I was looking to fill a little time with some one-on-one contact. I invited the man into my office and we began the interview.

He came from another part of the country. I had never been there so I found it interesting listening to him go into his past while he also described the New England state where he had lived all his life. He told of the extreme poverty once you got away from the Atlantic coastline. As we visited, he shared that his wife and their son had traveled to Des Moines in order to start a new life together. (I would later learn that was not the complete truth. His home state had a much more aggressive policy for removing children from the home than Iowa did when neglect issues were turned in against the parents. They had really fled the state in an attempt to negate the removal of their child from their custody). But as the interview went on, he started to ask questions about *my* background, *my* family and why *I* had chosen to be a pastor. As we talked, something started to happen that did not often take place. God began moving in his life. I was able to share my faith journey and how faith affected my choices for living. That faith journey was the reason I found myself working at the Door as God continued to bless and teach me lessons I needed to learn.

Several days later he returned to my office, wanting to again visit about God. As I explained that God loved him and his family and had a plan for them that might still be hard to grasp, he was moved by that possibility. He came to a point, when we spoke of forgiveness, where he asked if he might accept this gift of God's love for himself. I shared several scriptures and in his own words he asked God to enter his life. We finished that time and he then asked me what has become a troubling theological question: "*CAN GOD FORGIVE SIN*"? We had been there for quite a long time and I offered the acceptable answer, "*OF COURSE.*"

It was at this point in our emerging relationship that he decided to get real with me and in the process, God started to speak to my heart about what I could learn if I only were willing to spend the time with these folks. He then defined his question. "*Bob*", he said, *"I have killed a man and I wondered if this accepting Jesus thing really means that God has forgiven me?"* Wow! I still believe that God was working in his life seeking to offer forgiveness as well as helping him learn to do the right thing. My day changed at that moment. I then invited him to share with me at which time he became very defensive. It became apparent over the next few days that he had never been caught for the crime.

The following is an account of that experience.

He had worked for a factory owner in a New England state as a laborer. But he had an interesting side profession. He liked to start fires and had been hired over the years as an arsonist to torch buildings so the owners could collect insurance payments. It worked well for him. He got money and the owner collected the insurance, ending unprofitable business ventures at the same time. He told me had done one stint in prison for his activities and it was so bad that he was never going back to prison.

The story unfolded that he had been contacted by the owner of a warehouse to torch it on a given night for the insurance money. But in between the time of the contract and the fire, another employee had gotten into a fight with the owner. Money was tight for the business and the owner apparently had not paid the person what he owed him for his wages. In a public area this other employee threatened to burn down the building along with some other threats against the owner if his demands were not met.

It was several weeks later that the fire was set and the fire department arrived to fight the blaze. In the process of fighting the blaze, one of the fire fighters lost his life. It did not take the local police long to determine the motive for the blaze and to bring charges against the disgruntled employee. The legal process being what it is, the innocent person was convicted and at the time of conversation, was doing prison time for the arson and death of a fire fighter who was carrying out his duties.

The whole experience with Jesus, and who knows

what else, had so unsettled the man that he truly wanted to seek forgiveness and then began to ask what he might do to reduce his guilt and help get the innocent person out of prison. Although motivated by great intentions, and I believe the presence of God, his conviction to stay out of prison was stronger. He absolutely refused to take responsibility for his actions. He also continually sought my assurance that I could not and would not break confidence and turn him in to the authorities. (I want to tell you I had a number of sleepless nights in dealing with the fact that a man was in prison who should not be there. The other struggle was my responsibility as a pastor to protect the sacredness of the confessional).

I never did report any of this to the police, nor would I have done so, but he was unable to trust me with his life. Come to think of it, I am not sure what I would have done, either, had I been in his shoes. I remember times in my own life when God's spirit has broken into places I would just have soon God left alone, and I found myself spilling out pain and suffering that later I wondered why I had done it.

I made several calls that week to a friend who happened to be county attorney in one of the surrounding counties. I gave him details of the crime, and then asked if I had the location, the name of the person in prison and other details if that would be enough to raise questions about his innocence and help to get him released from prison. I was informed that unless the man came forward and admitted his part in the crime, no one would take up the case. I learned something of the justice system that day. I was told they had a conviction. A person was paying for the crime. No one would open up the possibility the wrong person was there on my information unless I wanted to give up the individual who had confessed. I could not do that as a pastor.

I continued to share with the guilty man that forgiveness also demands making amends for our actions. This is not so much a requirement of forgiveness but it is a direct result of what we feel once we have experienced that forgiveness. It became apparent that he was truly sorry but he was equally resolved not to come forward when it would cost him prison time. When I returned to work the next day, I found out that he had left town. I also found out that the Department of Human Services had caught up with them and had made efforts to return the child to his home state.

It is a funny thing with God, isn't it?

God takes us at the very place we are in our life at the moment He finds us. God loves us and pours out His grace upon us that was made real in Jesus Christ. But once we step into God's presence, life changes. I believe it changed that day for the man who had just come into my office seeking a place to lay his head for a few days while they made plans to continue their flight from life. We gave them a glimpse into how much God loved them and their family. They spent Labor Day at our home along with some other men from the Mission. We put our feet under the table and shared a meal. We played with their little son. I came to care for both him and his spouse. I often wonder what happened to them.

Did they every stop running?

Did he ever find conviction so troubling that he came forward and took the place of the man in prison as Jesus took his place on the cross?

I don't know the answers to those questions, but I do know one thing.

When somebody asks me today if God can forgive sin, I no longer give them the pat answer of "*SURE!*" But instead, I pull up a chair and invite them into conversation with me, knowing that I won't be making my next appointment anytime soon.

When God breaks into our lives we best be ready to respond.

God has two dwellings - one in heaven, the other in meek and thankful hearts.
                    -Izaak Walton

A Bike Ride to Remember

I have come to enjoy reading love stories over the years. One of my favorite writers is Nicholas Sparks. I find myself having a hard time putting down one of his books until I have finished reading it. One of his titles, *"A Walk to Remember,"* is one such love story. I have seen in my career as a minister many love stories played out in the lives of my parishioners. One such couple will probably never provide the material for Sparks to write about but they did touch my life.

I officially started working as the Skywalk Chaplain in downtown Des Moines in an office space provided free of charge by the management company that controls the skywalk system. My start date was January of 1993, although I had been volunteering there for the past several months as Jerry Ulin (the previous Skywalk Chaplain) moved to early retirement. It was mid-January when I first met this couple; they were in their early forties. Tom & Mary (not their real names) found themselves homeless on the streets of Des Moines. They had taken up shelter in Churches United.

In the early days of the Churches United Shelter, they were moving residents between five participating churches during the winter months. This shelter had been set up to prevent any more people from dying of exposure during the cold months of the year. As with many of the homeless, they spent a great deal of time wandering the skywalk system of Des Moines in order to keep warm and to just have something to do. For whatever reason, they found their way into my office. We began the process of becoming acquainted as I was also beginning to learn that meeting the needs of people on the streets would be much more difficult than I had at first anticipated.

As we visited over the coming days, I recall asking Mary what it was she needed and would like if I could secure the item for her. She thought a moment and then responded, *"I would like a Bible."* That was clearly one of the easiest requests to honor that I would have in my time at the Door of Faith Mission. I also remember thinking that if I were homeless, I doubt a Bible would be my first request for assistance. (That probably speaks a bit more about my faith than I like to admit, looking back).

They started to let their story unfold. They had both come from Omaha the past fall in order to escape some destructive relationships they had been involved with there. Neither of them had a car or a driver's license for that matter. It had taken them two weeks to ride their bicycles from Omaha to Des Moines. They would make ten or so miles a day and then camp alongside the road or in a city park as they sought food from churches along the way. In the past, I had folks stop by the church seeking assistance when I was serving a local church but I had never really taken the time to get to know them. I would either offer them assistance or refuse the request. It has become much more difficult for me to say no to people since my time at the Mission.

Some of the agencies that got involved with them felt it best if Mary had been placed in an institution, but there was reluctance on both their parts to let that happen. Neither had any money, nor means of support at the time. Mary would eventually qualify for SSDI (Social Security Disability Income), which would open up housing options that clearly were out of reach for them at the time. I remember helping them navigate those channels and how frustrating it was watching the government agencies work (or not work, as one might conclude). Over a period of time they were able to find housing, offering them safety from the streets. In order to have spending money they

126

would "can" each day. (I remember the first time one of the homeless told me they had a canning job and I asked them where the canning company was located in Des Moines). I would come to understand that it meant they had a daily route they walked in which they went through the trash bins downtown seeking cans people had tossed out that could be redeemed for five cents a can. On a good day they might get $8-10, which would then allow them to purchase smokes and other items.

One day they came into the office and asked if I would be willing to perform their marriage ceremony? I was reluctant to do marriage ceremonies while working at the Mission. Over the years I questioned the commitment of folks who came wanting me to perform their marriages in order to avoid paying a judge their required fee. I was honored, though, to be asked to share in Tom and Mary's ceremony. We made arrangements with the Mission to use the chapel area in the afternoon for their wedding. The Door of Faith Mission cook also agreed to make a wedding cake and punch as his gift to the couple. He knew them from Faith Café (the free meal each day for non-residents) which provided their noon meal. This actually provided their only balanced meal of the day, for that matter.

Mary had several friends from Churches United's board of directors who agreed to get her a dress, and also have her hair done. I remember seeing her and being frankly shocked by the way she appeared with use of some makeup and nice clothes. Tom also had a bit of luck in acquiring a new suit. It seemed that the man upstairs in the apartment building had recently died and Tom had been able to secure his suit, which became the groom's wedding suit. They were married that afternoon at 3:00 o'clock in the Mission's Chapel. Tom was so overcome with emotion that he was unable to speak his vows and stood there crying for a while, attempting to find composure. I, along with the other eight or so people, also found tears streaming from our eyes as well. It was during the reception that someone inquired as to where the groom had gone. The cook called me to the back door and said the groom was going through the garbage behind the Mission. It was apparently the time they made their canning run each day and just getting married did not seem a reason to give up a whole day's work.

This couple would remain a part of our lives. In fact, shortly after moving to Windsor United Methodist Church, I got a call from Mary telling me that Tom was sick from a stroke and in the hospital. He had experienced a stroke a few months before in which his speech became slurred, but from which he soon recovered. He had a real fear of hospitals and a day had gone by after the stroke before Mary called the ambulance, assuming Tom was just resting and would get to feeling better. He did not improve and went to hospice. I would also be a part of the death process with this family. I had found at Dallas Center, where I was the pastor for nine years, that it was not uncommon to have different services for members of my congregation. That would become the same at the Mission as I found ways to be in ministry with these folks, and as they ministered unto me as well.

Faith has remained a part of Mary's life as she continues to attend church and grow in her faith and mature. I'm not sure but she may have touched people's lives more than we have touched hers over the years.

When we look at people downtown who are presently living on the streets, what do you think:

Do you wonder about their families?

Do you wonder why they came to be homeless in Des Moines?

Do you wonder when was the last time somebody stopped and visited with them other than another person who is homeless?

Do you wonder what they might have to teach if you only had the time or desire to find out?

Or do you just hope you can get by them without their making eye contact with you and asking for something? Don't worry, most of the homeless have learned to steer clear of others and with any luck they become invisible, blending into the surroundings. Visibility will bring attention that they do not seek, and in most cases problems they cannot handle.

So the parade of life continues each day on the streets of Des Moines and across this country. The fortunate go to work and then return home. The homeless just hope to pass the time and maybe for a moment find some expression of love that is so sadly missing from their lives.

If there is love in the heart, there will be beauty in the character. If there is beauty in the character, there will be harmony in the home. If there is harmony in the home, there will be order in the nation. When there is order in the nation, there will be peace in the world.

-Old Proverb

Christmas Is About Giving

Christmas was always an extremely busy time at the Mission. Not only did the men have needs physically and emotionally at this time of the year, but so did many people who came to us with needs for food and gifts. We also had a commitment to the men to attempt to provide for them items above and beyond what they normally received so they might know of Jesus' extravagant love of them.

It was Christmas eve day late in the afternoon. Julie had come down to the office with a friend and her infant in order to have one of the men work on the friend's car. This friend was low income and had an older child who was in a day-care at the time. Many of the men at the mission had different gifts and professions, not the least of those being car mechanics.

We had one man, who I will call Dave, who had been at the Mission for four or so months. Dave had also been there many times before so we had built a relationship with him during the times he remained sober. In conversation with Dave, this woman's situation had come up. We explained that she was working full time but was also going through a divorce and had two children. Things were not going well for her financially as well, and Christmas had made it much more difficult. To top things off, she had an old car that she was having difficulty keeping running. Dave offered to work on the car for free if she could get it down to the Mission. Several weeks before he had spent an afternoon adjusting the carburetor on her car and making other corrections in the hope that it would keep running. The car did run better but was still stalling on her from time to time.

It was that mechanical problem that brought her to

the Mission that day to have her car adjusted before picking up her other child from day-care. Dave was outside working on the car. Julie and the mom, along with her infant, were in another office. I was on the phone with a mom who had no gifts for Christmas that year, trying to make arrangements before we left in a half hour to go home and have dinner with our family before heading out to the Christmas eve service at our church.

One of the men from the Mission came in and said, *"Bob, we have an emergency outside and need you right away."* I informed him I was on the phone with a woman who needed help and could not come out. He persisted, *"Bob, you need to come now. Dave has wrecked the woman's car."* That got my attention.

We went outside to see what could possibly have happened. The car was a block away, with the hood rammed through a building downtown. Piecing it together, this is what happened: Dave had one foot on the gas pedal, and the other on the ground beside the door. He was standing up outside the car at the same time, giving the engine gas so he could determine why it was missing. For some reason he had the car in drive, and apparently had fixed the stalling problem. The car took off and jumped the cement by the parking lot, and in the process knocked him to the ground.

Somehow it went clear through a parking lot without hitting any other cars, with Dave in hot pursuit, once he picked himself up off the ground. It then jumped the sidewalk, missing the parking meter, crossed 11th street downtown without meeting up with any other cars. It crossed a sidewalk, missing the parking meters, and then with the hood up, rammed itself through a basement window on an abandoned building. The momentum ripped the hood off the car, took out the grill and totally destroyed the engine. It came to rest, but before stopping rolled backwards pinning the driver door open on the parking meter it had barely missed. This is the sight I saw when I got outside, along with a lot of men standing around shaking their heads.

My next task was to go back inside and inform this woman that she no longer had a car that functioned or had any possibility of running. How would she be able to get to her job after Christmas? What would she do for a car? She had hoped with her income tax refunds in April to purchase a different car but this one needed to get her through until that time. It was apparent that would not happen. I went inside and told Julie we needed to talk. When I shared the story with her, she asked me, "*Who is going to tell her?*" My pastoral response, "*She is your friend.*" The woman took the news and then went outside, but before that she asked one question. "*Did anybody get hurt?*" And her first comment to Dave after she saw the car was, "*This is not worth drinking over and it was not your fault.*" I will assure you the men at the Mission were not that kind to Dave with the comments they made over the next few weeks.

Julie and I realized we needed to take her to pick up her child and then get them home. Her son asked when he got in the car, "*Mommy, where is our car?*" She assured him they would visit about that when they got home. We made plans for Christmas day for transportation for her and her family before heading home for Christmas eve dinner. We had a long discussion on the way home as to how we might raise money immediately to purchase another car. Thoughts such as asking our church to take an offering. Calling the Mission Board of Directors for money. Like most Christians, we did what most folks do in such a circumstance. I tried to figure out ways to fix the problem by having others pay the cost. It became apparent that no one had money to solve the situation or any really great ideas.

The next day Julie said that she thought we should visit for a while. This idea should have been mine but it was my wife who I believe spoke for God. She said, "*Bob, you know we both have a car and we also have an extra car for the children to drive to and from school.*" Her suggestion was that we give my car to the lady for a time until she could purchase her own car. It was decided that when I had to drive, I could take the children's car and they could ride the bus, but most of the time Julie suggested we ride to work together and I could take the bus downtown from Merle Hay Road. It would be that the ride from Adel (where we lived at that time) to Des Moines gave us time to visit and share one-another's company. The bus ride would give me time to make new friends on the bus. Our old car would become a great vehicle for this family. The car was not really beautiful but it was reliable. It happened in the spring she did in fact get her tax refund and turned the title of our car back to us.

The episode with Dave taught me some real lessons.

The poor, unlike myself who had money, are more concerned with people and their feelings than those like me who are concerned with our possessions.

The opportunity of sharing our car began to reflect the options of sacrificial giving in my life and allowed me to see how God blesses us through faith in Him.

I came to understand that when there is a need, a Christian should not pass the buck to somebody else to fix. Rather, God calls us to take inventory of what we have been given and how those resources might be used to bless another if we place them in God's hand.

The mom went on with her life with little interruption. Dave on the other hand would continue to drink and struggle with his life. Even today, he continues the dying process of alcoholism. But I also learned that

136

though we struggle with issues that really destroy our lives, we still have gifts we can give to others. I also learned that others can touch us when we open ourselves to the presence of God in our midst.

Kindness is the golden chain by which society is bound together.
-Johann Wolfgang von Goethe

The Personal Cost of Homelessness

One day at the Door of Faith Mission I found this poem (hand written on an old piece of paper), in some belongings of a resident who had left everything behind. It pretty well sums up the high cost of being homeless and on the streets.

Day after day
I live in vain
Because I smoke
Crack, cocaine

Day after day
I live my life
My mind confused
By stress and strife

Why oh why
Do I do these things
That make me forsake
My wedding ring?

Out of my home
Livin' on the street
No warm bed
No food to eat

I want to put a face to that type of despair. Mac happened to show up at the Mission one day seeking a place to stay. One of the Broadlawns outreach workers had brought him to us, wondering if we had a bed available for

him. He looked like a wild man possessed by demons.
Mac had been living downtown under the bridge on Grand
Avenue, just next to the YMCA. He had not had a shower
in a month. Meals had been few and far between. He had
open sores all over his body from a reaction to some
medication he had been taking. And he was just plain
mean. In fact, the outreach worker cautioned us about
being alone with him due to his violent behavior. We were
told that he had attacked the worker in the van one day
when the worker refused to give him what he needed. With
all the reasons to not take him, we did.

In the next few months the story began to unfold as
Mac started to trust those of us working at the Mission. He
had been on his own since a young child. The state had
bounced him from foster home to foster home until he was
finally old enough to be on his own. He had learned to care
for himself and take care of his own needs, seldom open to
trusting anyone. Mac had built up walls to protect himself
from anyone getting too close again and in turn his life was
a mess.

He started to work odd jobs. He also started to
attend chapel services and ultimately he would begin
attending a local church. Six months later you would not
have recognized him as the same person who came by the
front door seeking a place to live. In fact, he would attend
"Promise Keepers," along with 23 other men from the
Mission, when it was held in Des Moines that year. He
was one of the first to go forward during the altar call.
Actually, he got up the minute the person started to speak
and sat in front of the pulpit for 30-plus minutes before the
altar call was ever issued. He started something in that
others joined him on the floor, waiting to deal with
problems in their lives.

We saw such great things that Mac was asked to
move to our halfway houses located on Buchanan Street in

Des Moines, along with the other seven men living there. He continued to make progress and had by then secured a full-time job and was working and saving money. Mac was almost ready to move out when he made one mistake (I believe he did this on purpose to sabotage his progress in the hope of staying on at the Mission). He had bought a car and was working on getting his license re-instated. Mac had about another two-three weeks before he could go to the DOT and take the driving tests. Unfortunately, he started driving the car without a legal license. The men living in of the houses informed me of his actions. We discussed the issues one Sunday afternoon at the house meeting and I told him that if he drove again without a license he would have to move out. The next week he missed the house meeting and his car was gone from the back parking lot. He had intentionally challenged the house rules and by his actions put the other men at risk in their recovery.

The other staff asked me if I wanted them to go to the house so I would not be alone when I told him to pack up his belongings and move out. (We all remembered his personality when he arrived at the Mission and the warning that we should not be alone with him). I would truly have liked to take another staff person with me, but I was unwilling to give up the authority the men placed in me by having them believe I would not enforce the rules equally. I still recall that day when I asked Mac to leave. It was truly a sad day for both of us. I was betting that my relationship with him was enough to provide for my safety along with my faith that God would care for me.

A few months earlier I had stood between him and another man in the houses when he had threatened to kill this individual. It became apparent that Mac had been set up and he had seen me deal with this conflict when I took his side. He would years later tell me that he thought I

143

must have a black belt in that I showed no fear when I confronted him. In the Bible, God says, *"that perfect love casts out fear."* In our lives there comes a day when we have to decide, either I will trust God or I won't. Several weeks later, Mac dumped on me by saying, *"I was doing well until you kicked me out and that caused my relapse."*

I would find over the years that decisions we make do affect others. The halfway houses were run with one assumption: Grace is a great thing, but there is none here. Each man's sobriety in those houses depended upon all of them living in covenant. It would prove difficult for them to live in covenant, and yet that same covenant that was so difficult to keep would change many of their lives as they grew to love and trust others.

One Sunday years later, Mac and his finance showed up at a worship service in the church I am now serving as pastor. He wanted Julie and me to know he was doing fine and also wanted to introduce the woman to whom he was engaged. There would be many more times when men would return and tell me or another staff member that when they were forced to look at themselves by a decision I had to make, was the time they realized how their life had become so out of control.

In Des Moines, we had been seeing a number of signs attached to light poles as families attempted to find lost pets. The signs would describe the cat or dog and then include a phone number where the person could reach them if they found the pet.

The following sign appeared on a light pole on the north side of Des Moines just before the holiday seasons and shows what happens when lives are lived outside of God's protection:

LOST - DADDY
PLEASE God, Find my Daddy -

Tell Him I love Him and Miss Him
O O O X X X

This sign was hung beside a Quick Trip outlet (convenience store chain in Des Moines), where hundreds of people drove past it daily.

These men are not just homeless men, they are somebody's parent or child or spouse. I would learn that the families suffered just as much as did the person who found himself homeless and on the streets. The next time you drive by a homeless person on your way home at night, pray for them and the family that misses them so dearly. Pray for the Macs of the world, that they may find the love in God they have so missed growing up. Pray that just possibly you may even be the one that God chooses to show this love.

He who sees farther than others can give the world vision; he who stands steadier than others can give it character; he who forgets himself in doing things for others can give it religion.

-Arthur T. Hadley

Who Is God?

Several years after I started working at the Mission it was decided that the Mission should offer some type of recovery program in-house. The acronym "STAR" was given to this program. "STAR" stood for spiritual training and recovery. Those men who signed up and were accepted for the "STAR" program were given better living accommodations and other benefits in exchange for a six-month commitment of their life.

One of the hopes was that the men would make a personal commitment to Jesus Christ during that time at the Mission. We did a spiritual inventory for each man. The purpose of this inventory was to help the staff working with the man to better understand his individual faith background. It was also helpful to gather some insight into what place God might already play in their lives. It was also hoped they would come to rely upon God for not only maintaining sobriety but also assist them as they attempted to create a new life for themselves.

As the Chaplain at the mission it was decided I should be the one who did the spiritual inventories with each man. When the inventory was completed, the man would then be assigned to a case worker who was to meet minimally once a week with him. One such man ("Bill") had complete honesty as he shared his responses to my questions. His honesty also helped me come to a better understanding of how much we in the faith community take for granted about the knowledge of the world pertaining to God. I hope you enjoy the responses.

I asked Bill to tell me of his church background. It seemed easier for men to speak about where they attended church than to converse about the place God has in their life. Bill told me that he was baptized Lutheran. His parents had taken him to a church nearby and that seemed the reason they chose the Lutheran Church. He continued, *"My mom was Methodist so we attended a Methodist Church for a couple of years when I was in second or third grade."* He jumped at this point to his senior year in high school. It was during this time in his life that his mom moved away with her third husband. He had chosen to remain behind in order to finish school that senior year instead of moving to a new high school. The family that took him happened to be Roman Catholic. The father of this family told him he had to attend if he wished to live with them and finish school, so he found himself attending a Roman Catholic Church his senior year of high school. He then gave me the answer I was seeking, *"I don't go any longer because I don't find it pleasuring or rewarding."*

It was also helpful to find out what scripture background the men had. It was not unusual for them to have a fairly good grasp of scripture. I also found over the years that the many of the men had memorized a large portion of scripture before they arrived at the Mission. It was also evident that just because they had memorized the scripture, one did not want to assume they understood it or followed it.

So my next question was, *"Tell me of your favorite scripture or Bible story."* This allowed the men again to reveal in a non-threatening way the place of scripture in their lives. It was much like planning a funeral in the local church for a person who had never attended. When I as the pastor would ask them for scripture to be used in the service, it was not uncommon for them to ask me to pick out one since they could recall no passage from scripture that had any meaning in their lives. On the other hand, some of the men would go into great detail telling me what passages they enjoyed and what those passages meant in their lives. Hopefully, you begin to see how that information might be used over the next six months as we worked individually with each man.

Bill was quick to respond to my question about his favorite scripture, *"I don't know any."* There was some silence and it was evident he was thinking of the question. He then responded, *"I like the Christmas story where the three kings traveled to _____ "*, (there was a pause*)*. *"Wasn't it Bethlehem to see the baby Jesus who lived in a little grey hut? I think he was born there. I believe the kings followed the north star to see where he lived. I don't read the Bible much, but I have watched the old and new movies about Jesus."*

I then asked him when he read the Bible? His response was something to the effect that he read the GIDEON Bible. At least that was the word on the Bible.

I asked him if something happened to him and death interrupted his life today, did he think he would go to heaven? Bill replied, *"Who's to say?"* We continued to visit about Jesus. I spoke a bit about God's love made known through Jesus. I commented that God's plan was for us to find eternal life by accepting Jesus as our Savior. And then I asked Bill if he had ever done that?

"I went on a retreat to Colfax, it was kind of like a monastery. During the retreat I did my 4th & 5th step. It was during this time several men told me I should get down on my knees and ask forgiveness. I was really_____ off to have them tell me to do that. Then the guy said I could go up to my room and kneel by the bed and do it. That is what I did."

Bill had a good heart. Bill also had no idea what we were talking about when it came to the Bible, but he was receptive. He would eventually find a church and started to attend its services. He continued to stay sober. As far as I know he has not ventured back into the old lifestyle he had spent so many years in. That is nothing short of a miracle when you consider his life story.

One day he asked for help. Some woman had named him in a paternity suit. She claimed he was the father of her child and wanted to collect child support. He could not remember her very clearly and doubted he was the father. I recall when the test returned and they stated there was a 99.9% chance he was the father, Bill was ecstatic. To his way of thinking, that meant there was a .1% chance he was not the father so he was off the hook. When I explained the system and how it worked he quickly went from euphoria to despair. To the best of his recollections he might have had sex with 75-100 women in his life and just could not remember them all. Many of whom he had picked up in the bars and only knew for a short amount of time. His physical appearance had me wondering how he got 75 women to go home with him, let alone one. I believe from the time he entered the Mission he also stopped the extra sexual encounters. Quite a change for a person who for so long only thought of his own needs above others.

It was in a Bible study one evening and we were speaking about the act of piety. The topic of fasting came up as one form that some of the men had tried. Bill sat quietly and listened to the conversation. He truly enjoyed eating and I had little suspicion that he would experiment with fasting. Eventually, though, he did venture to ask a question. *"If I give up sex for 24 hours, does that count as fasting?"* Julie was a bit red faced as she struggled to hold back her laughter. The rest of the men were not so compassionate.

Bill had a way of speaking whatever was on his mind. He lacked some social graces. But it was refreshing to see a person so interested in the new life that he had entered that nothing was off limits to him. He had an openness to asking questions. In the process I also truly

152

believe he came to a personal encounter with God that brought change to his life and hope for the future.

I would invite you to consider how we speak with folks who are non-churched.

They don't know or understand the terms we throw around.

They may have heard the Bible stories, but probably not.

They may have an interest in God, but can quickly be turned off by our remarks.

So how do you share the Good News with people who have no idea of who Jesus is or what God is doing through him?

These are interesting encounters that challenge our ability to make God real. May God bless you with some Bills in the coming years. It is a wonderful thing to watch people grow from infancy in the faith to adulthood. Thanks for pushing me beyond my comfort level more than once, Bill. May God continue to bless you and sustain you in this life and in the life to come.

May God also pour His blessing out on each of you readers of this book and thanks for sharing some of my stories. God bless you.

Pastor Bob